WITH WINGS OF EAGLES

Sermons for the Easter Season Series A

Richard Carl Hoefler

WITH WINGS OF EAGLES

2352/ISBN 0-89536-624-X   PRINTED IN U.S.A.

Dedicated to
The Rev. Prof. J. B. Bedenbaugh, Ph.D.
whose knowledge of the Bible
is surpassed only by his
dedication to the Gospel

CONTENTS

He Is Here Now

THE RESURRECTION OF OUR LORD
EASTER DAY
John 20:1-9

Today we celebrate the most festive Sunday of the Church Year — Easter. We go all out. The organist sets the pace with a vigorous prelude of victory. The choir features its finest anthems of exultation. The hymns are triumphant and we sing them with gusto. The processional with its seasonal banners marches to the altar, flooded with the flickering lights of candles, and flowers fill the air with the fragrance of Spring. We appear for worship in our finest Easter fashions. It is a great and glorious occasion.

However, our Gospel for this morning stands in striking — if not stark — contrast to the high drama of this day. It is John's account of the Easter story, and it is quiet and subdued. There is some running of people back and forth to the tomb, but overall the tone of the text is calm and restrained — tranquil rather than triumphant. There are no angelic messengers, no shouts of "He is risen," no hallelujahs.

The text of our Gospel opens early on a Sunday morning. It is still dark. One lone woman makes her way to the tomb. Suddenly she stops. In the gray, hazy light of pre-dawn she sees that the stone in front of the tomb has been rolled away. Hurriedly, she turns and seeks out the disciples to tell them. So, John's account of the Easter story begins.

Three people participate in the drama that follows. Three people visit the tomb — three very different people, and they have three very different reactions.

The first is Mary Magdalene, a reformed lady of the night. Alone she comes to the tomb, and when she sees the stone has been rolled away, she jumps to the conclusion that someone has come during the night and stolen the body of Jesus, her friend. As one theologian puts it, for Mary this first act of the Easter story might be entitled, the "Case of the Missing Corpse." She is moved not to faith but to fear. Foul-play was afoot during the night, and some thieves have robbed the grave and taken the body of Jesus.

The second player in our drama is Peter. Mary finds him with another disciple, and she tells them the terrible news: "They have taken the Lord out of the tomb and we do not know where they have laid him." Peter is shocked. He says not a word. He looks at the other disciple. Can it be true? Immediately they run toward the tomb to see for themselves.

Then a very human note is added. The other disciple, being younger, outruns Peter and reaches the tomb first. It may have been that Peter was out of shape, or his age was telling on him, but whatever the reason, Peter lost the race to the tomb. However, what Peter lacked in athletic ability he made up for in sheer impulsiveness and raw courage. John may have outrun Peter — but Peter out-dared John.

When Peter arrives at the tomb, the other disciple had not gone in. Rather he was — as the Greek text indicates — "peeping into the tomb." He may have been afraid of contamination by a dead body or simply struck with awe. But not Peter. He brashly enters the tomb without hesitation. He sees that the tomb is empty. There is no body, only the linen wrappings lying where the body had been — and here is the amazing thing: All of this has no significance for Peter. He is satisfied that

Mary had spoken the truth. The body is gone. We have no indication of what went through Peter's mind, but there is no suggestion that he was impressed or brought close to belief. Luke tells us that Peter went home. All we can conclude from this record of Scriptures is that Peter not only lost the race to the tomb, but the significance of the empty tomb was lost to him.

The third player in the drama is the "Beloved Disciple," traditionally identified as John. He follows Peter into the tomb. Then the text says, "He saw and believed." Scholars have speculated about John's reaction. Why is it that he was the only one of the three who caught the significance of the missing body? Most think that the very presence of the burial clothes led John to the logical conclusion that the body had not been stolen. Grave robbers would not have taken the time to unwrap the corpse. They would have rushed in, grabbed the body and fled.

Other scholars suggest that the special relationship John had with Jesus enabled him to realize the significance of what he saw. His great love for Jesus and our Lord's particular love for him had given John a unique insight. But such a view denigrates and subordinates Mary and Peter to second-class status in their relationship with the Lord. This cannot be the case. Such speculations of what and why Mary, Peter and John did what they did lead us nowhere.

What we are really faced with in this little drama is the simple fact that three people visited the empty tomb and only one of them believed. One out of three found faith at the empty tomb. Not a very strong recommendation for the reality of the resurrection. If this is all the record we had of that first Easter morning, our resurrection faith would be based on a very shaky foundation.

The truth is, we have not one Easter story but four — Matthew's, Mark's, Luke's as well as John's. Each in his own way tells his own story. This, however, does not solve our problem but only adds to it, because the stories are so different. There are disagreements and contradictions among the Gospel writers as to who visited the tomb, how many, when and where.

While many exegetes and biblical scholars try to harmonize the resurrection narratives into one melodious ballad, their efforts generally end up sounding off-key. There are just too many diverse details to dovetail the various accounts into a neat and finished story of what actually happened on that first Easter day.

What, then, are we to conclude from the differing accounts and conflicting reactions of those who claim to have been present at the resurrection of our Lord?

To begin with, we need to sit loose as we listen, and realize that belief in the resurrection — the empty tomb — a risen body — has never been easy. It wasn't easy for the disciples who lived out the drama, or for the early Christians who first heard about it, and it is doubly difficult for us who must look back at it through two thousand years of history.

The resurrection of Jesus is a unique and singular event. It cannot be repeated or compared to any other similar occurrences in history. Like the virgin birth, the death of God on a cross, and the last supper with the disciples, our Lord's resurrection is unique and unparalleled. It is a divine mystery that no scholarly sleuth can unravel. Such once-and-for-all events are by their very nature incredible and impossible to prove.

To add to our dilemma, all of these stories in Scriptures about the empty tomb are after-the-fact. No one really witnessed the resurrection event; they only testified to the after-effects — the fall-out — of the event.

When Jesus was crucified, the hillside of Golgotha was swelling with people. Hundreds witnessed with their own eyes the brutal act of execution. The crucifixion was a most public event. But no one witnessed the resurrection. No one saw with his own eyes the stone being rolled back and the buried body of Christ emerge from the tomb. It all happened at night under the physical cover of darkness and the spiritual cover of divine intervention. All the first witnesses saw was a stone out of place, an empty tomb, and a pile of discarded grave clothes.

Is that it? Are we left with the resurrection as only a murky myth or at best an unintelligible mystery? No! The cumulative testimony of the historic church is that the visit to the empty tomb is not the way one comes to faith in the resurrection. Even when we add the more exotic accounts of the other Gospels with their angelic messengers, their shouts of, "He is risen," and their exulting hallelujahs, we are still left with a rather flimsy foundation for the fantastic proclamation that Jesus rose bodily from the grave. Rather, the testimony of the saints and martyrs of Christendom is that the resurrection faith is grounded in the *appearances of the resurrected Lord.* It is not *entering* the empty tomb, but *encountering* the living Lord that produced in the past and still produces today a belief in the resurrection of Jesus Christ our Lord.

Luther hits the nail on the head when he says, "We do not believe in the resurrection because of the empty tomb but because of the Christ-filled world."

The evidence of Scripture is that Mary and Peter, after their experiences of visiting the empty tomb, did come to believe, but only after an encounter with the risen Lord. John tells us that Jesus appeared to Mary in the grave-garden and she believed. Jesus appeared to Peter when the disciples were gathered together behind closed doors and Peter believed.

So we are led to faith, not by experiencing a year-by-year return to the empty tomb — retelling the story — and struggling to make sense of it. No! We, like all the faithful of history, come to true belief in the resurrection by encountering in our own lives the living Lord. It is not understanding the empty tomb but encountering the living Christ that creates in us a resurrection faith.

Paul did not visit the empty tomb, and yet his record is the earliest witness we have of the resurrection. In First Corinthians, Paul presents the basis for this belief. He writes:

> *He was raised to life on the third day according to the scriptures and he appeared to Cephas, and afterwards to the Twelve. Then he appeared to over five hundred of our brothers at once . . . Then he appeared to James . . . In the end he appeared even to me.*

Note, Paul does not push belief in the empty tomb. There is no mention of the stone rolled away or the discarded grave clothes. There is no appeal to believe the details of that first Easter morning. Paul simply stresses the appearance of the living Lord to Cephas, to the twelve, to the five hundred, to James and to himself.

For Paul the meaning of the resurrection is that the old world has passed away and a new age is breaking in upon us in the presence of Christ the Lord. Because we have communion with Christ, we have the only assurance possible of the factuality and the reality of an historic resurrection.

There is no proving of the resurrection, not by sacred stories of an empty tomb or detailed descriptions of discarded grave clothes. Not even the amazing case of the Shroud of Turin, examined for three years by forty scientists, working with their seventy-two crates of sophisticated twentieth-century instruments, can prove the resurrection as a fact of history. Only the appearance of the living Lord in our daily experiences can assure us that the resurrection is a reality.

How does Christ appear before us today? How can we

experience an encounter with the risen Lord today? The theological answer usually given is that by means of the word and sacraments we can encounter Christ. When the word is read and preached and witnessed to, and when the sacraments are rightly administered, Christ *comes.* He enters into history, intervenes into our world, enters into our lives, confronts us, and we encounter him.

There is, however, a more pastoral and personal answer to the question of how we encounter Christ. It is that Christ comes to us each day when we participate in the life, the new life given to us in our baptism and our resulting status as the children of God. The living Lord comes to us in our day-by-day experiences of forgiveness, freedom and fellowship.

Forgiveness

First, *forgiveness.* We encounter Christ as living Lord when we do wrong and cry out for mercy and experience the forgiving love of God. The resurrected Christ is our guaranteed absolution. He is our living declaration of grace. He is our continuous baptism, flowing like a river of pure water cleansing us daily from the dirt and filth that stains our lives. We know daily in the refreshment of his forgiveness that he has truly risen. Because we are forgiven, he has risen.

Freedom

Second, *freedom.* We encounter Christ as the living Lord when we experience liberation from the law. When we place our lives into the hands of our Savior, the burden and demands of endless laws and rules and regulations no longer weigh us down with the worry of wondering if we have been good enough and have done enough to please our Father God. As Christ took upon himself our sins, we take upon ourselves his righteousness, his goodness, his obedience. We are set free, not by an empty grave, but by his full grace. The crushing load of legal morality is lifted from our lives — the burden of petty piety falls from our backs, and we are *free*. This glad and glorious feeling of freedom is our assurance that we have encountered the living Lord who has defeated death, has risen from the grave and is with us now.

Fellowship

Third, *fellowship*. We encounter Christ as living Lord when we experience the fellowship within the Body of Christ, the church. The church is more than a pious in-group — a polite society of the respectable. The Church is a fellowship of saints, reborn sinners for whom Christ has died and in whom Christ lives. The church is not a spiritual union of dis-embodied souls. It is a flesh-and-blood fellowship of warm bodies that can be reached out to and touched.The church is a living organism. Christ is the head and we are the body. Christ is the bridegroom and we are the bride. Christ is the vine and we are the branches.We are grafted together by grace. We are in Christ and he is in us. We are *one* in Christ.

We need to remember that "raised" does not merely mean to be lifted up from the grave; it also means "exalted." The resurrection of Christ means we have been rescued from death, but it means so much more. It means that together with Christ and with each other, we are lifted up to a new and better life. This belonging, this feeling of being lifted up each day by one who loves us and cares for us as he cares for himself, this is our most important assurance that Easter is real.

The resurrected life of forgiveness, freedom and fellowship forms the basis of our belief in the resurrection, not a yearly visit to the empty tomb, no matter how much we dress up this day with special music, impressive processionals, trumpets, banners and lilies. The day-by-day participation in the risen and living Lord through the experiences of word and sacrament and the warm personal experiences of forgiveness, freedom and fellowship are the true foundation of our faith and our absolute, undeniable assurance that Christ has risen and that Christ is risen now.

An English bishop writes in his autobiography that when he was a little boy, he visited with friends too long and had to walk home alone at night through a dark forest.

In the daytime this wooded area was a place of great beauty and many fascinating wonders of nature, but at night it was a frightening place filled with strange noises, eerie shadows and ominous, shapeless figures.

The farther the little boy walked into the dense forest, the deeper the darkness became and the greater and more terrifying his fear.

Then in the distance ahead of him, he saw a faint flicker of light. As it came closer down the path, he guessed that it was a lantern. But who was carrying it? He had heard stories of highway men and bandits, frequenting the forest, encountering little boys, kidnapping them and carrying them off, never to be seen again.

Fear clutched at every fiber of his being. In panic he ran from the path and hid behind a tree. His heart was beating so hard he was sure the noise of it would betray his hiding place.

The stranger approached. He was now only a few steps away. The little boy almost fainted with fear, and as he caught his balance, he stepped to one side, and a twig snapped beneath his foot.

With that, the figure on the road stopped and called out, "Is that you son?" It was the voice of his father. The little boy rushed out and embraced him. "I thought you might get lost in the darkness," the father went on, "so I came out to meet you and walk you home."

The little boy took his father's hand, and together they walked home through the darkness, which was lighted now not only by the lantern but by the loving hand held tightly in the grip of a frightened little boy.

The bishop goes on to say that the experience of that night is forever in his memory, and the lesson it taught he has never forgotten. It is the simple truth that faith is not being unafraid in the darkness, but faith is knowing that we are not alone despite our fear of darkness.

This is the message of Easter. This is the meaning of the resurrection. It is not the casting out of all fears and doubts, nor is it the promise of no darkness; rather it is the assurance that because Christ is risen, we are not alone. In him we have forgiveness, freedom and fellowship.

Therefore, this Easter day we proclaim with great confidence, "Jesus is risen, resurrected from the dead. We are certain, for he is with us now!"

A Better Way

SECOND SUNDAY OF EASTER
John 20:19-31

We frequently make life difficult for ourselves. Perhaps this happens because we are so often fickle, inconsistent and changeable. We rejoice when we should be afraid, and we are terrified when there is every reason for great joy. This is so true of the Easter stories. In all the Gospel accounts, they begin with tears, blindness and doubts. The people who were privileged to visit the garden on that first Easter morning were terrified at the empty grave, at the angels, and at the risen Christ.

When Jesus entered Jerusalem with his face set toward the cross, the people greeted him with joy and shouting. When he rose victoriously from the grave, they met him with despair and doubt and fear.

This is particularly true of our Gospel for this morning. It is a drama filled with contradictions, mixed emotions and swiftly altered attitudes. It begins with the disciples gathered behind closed and bolted doors. Suddenly Jesus appears among them and their reaction quickly changes from fright to joy.

Christ greets them with a blessing of peace, and then shows them the wounds and scars of his battle with the Evil One. He immediately follows this with the gift of the Holy Spirit, and at the same time challenges them with the command to go forth into all the world and forgive fallen people of their sins. According to John's record, in one brief day, the disciples had experienced Easter, the

risen body of their Lord, Pentecost, and the Great
Commission. No wonder the disciples had mixed
emotions of joy and fear.

Amazingly, however, all of this high drama has been
historically up-staged by the more personal performance
of Thomas who dampens the whole drama of the day with
his doubt. Historically, the church, when examining this
passage recorded by John, has turned the spotlight of
attention on Thomas and his actions. His doubt has so
captured the imagination that in our popular language,
the phrase, "Doubting Thomas," has become the cliché,
the platitude, the stereotype for all unbelievers — and
this, despite the fact that most contemporary scholars
feel it is an unfortunate and unfair judgment against the
character of Thomas. One writer goes so far as to say that
if Thomas were alive today, he would have an open-and-
shut case to sue for slander.

Therefore, let us take a moment and look at the facts
concerning this much maligned man named Thomas.

The first three Gospels tell us nothing about Thomas
except to mention his name as one of the disciples; it is in
the Fourth Gospel that Thomas becomes the character we
commonly associate with the attitude of doubt.

In the Fourth Gospel, Thomas is usually referred to
as "Thomas who is called Didymus." "Thomas" in
Hebrew, and "Didymus" in Greek, are both words that
mean "twin." Today Thomas is familiar to us as a
personal name, but not so among the people at the time
of Christ. It was for them a nickname attached to the real
name of a person. Scholars tell us this apostle's name was
Judas, and Syrica sources, for example, refer to him as
"Judas Thomas," or "Judas the twin." This being true, it
is easy to understand why the Scriptures would refer to
him only as Thomas. They wanted to avoid confusing the
doubter with the betrayer.

The interesting fact is that no where in all of
Scriptures is Thomas referred to as "The Doubter"; this

is a designation tradition has given to him. Justified or not, the title has stuck. A single, vividly related incident has been enough to label this disciple as "Doubting Thomas" and has made of him a prototype of every person who has ever expressed an uncertainty or a doubt.

As we mentioned before, many biblical authorities dispute the fairness of this title, "doubter," and attempt to defend the degraded reputation of poor old Thomas. They point out that even though he begins by doubting our Lord's post-resurrection appearance, he ends up stating the supreme christological pronouncement of the Fourth Gospel, if not of all Scriptures — "My Lord and my God."

Like the story of the Tortoise and the Hare, Thomas is a slow starter in the race to belief compared to the other disciples, but in the end, he pulls out ahead of all the others and is the first to call Christ, "God." The disciples had addressed Jesus as Rabbi, Messiah, Prophet, King and even, Son of God, but it was Thomas who took the honor of being the first to call Jesus, "God."

Now why this contradiction of character? Why this drastic change in Thomas from stereotyped doubter to sensational confessor among the believers? To begin with, we need to see that it was not doubt that characterized Thomas as much as it was his demands. It was not his incredulity, his disbelief, his skepticism that surfaced in Scriptures, as much as it was his brash ultimatums — his demands.

Like the rest of the disciples, Thomas was not trained to be a rabbi let alone a religious leader. He probably had little education, but what he had learned was by practical experience in the so-called school of hard knocks. He had lived all his life close to the earth, and talk of spiritual realities came hard to Thomas. He had a keen sense of facts based on what could be seen and touched.

Many writers refer to Thomas as a skeptic, and to

some extent this is true. However, a skeptic is the type of person who prays,

> *O God, if there be a God,*
> *Save my soul, if I have a soul,*
> *and make me good, if there is*
> *such a thing as goodness.*

Such uncertainty never marked the opinions of Thomas. He seldom wavered; rather, he was a man of strong opinions concerning what he thought was true and what he was convinced was the right thing to do in a particular situation. In fact, Thomas is presented in the Scriptures as the one who interrupts the flow of action with his own ideas of what should be done.

When Jesus was called to go to the side of a sick and dying Lazarus (John 11:1-16), the trip involved going in the direction of Jerusalem where the Jewish authorities were determined that Jesus should die. In the minds of most of the disciples to answer this appeal and go to Lazarus would be a suicidal act of recklessness.But Thomas stood alone against them and demanded, "Let us also go, that we may die with him." This was not the action of a doubter; this was a decisive decision — a daring demand — of a very determined man.

In the Upper Room when Jesus was explaining to the disciples (John 14:1-6) the inevitability of the cross, his suffering and death, and the dangerous and difficult way that lay beyond the cross, Thomas once more interrupted, saying, "Lord, we know not whither thou goest: and how can we know the way?"

Again, not a statement of doubt, but a *demand* — a demand to know the precise details of the dangers and difficulties they would have to face.

A Man of Definite Demands

With these two examples before us of Thomas as a

man of definite demands, our Gospel for this morning takes on some revealing new insights.

John tells us in our text that Thomas was not with the disciples when Jesus appeared after his resurrection. So the disciples told Thomas, "We saw the Lord." Thomas answered, "If I do not see the scars of the nails in his hands, and put my finger where the nails were, and my hand in his side, I will not believe."

Such an expression is an expression of doubt, but it is a doubt, not of the fact of the resurrection, but of the mental state of the disciples. Thomas is challenging the reliability of the disciples' story. It is as if he were saying, "I wish I could believe *anything* as easily as you can believe *everything*. You say you saw our Lord's body present in this room; you were only seeing what you wanted to see. If the Lord had appeared to me, I would have demanded not only to see the Lord but to *touch* him. This would be proof-positive that he really had come back from the grave and was standing among you."

This mention of *touching the Lord* is very important. For Thomas was not asking to have the same experience as the disciples; he wanted *more*. He demanded not only to see the Lord, as the disciples had, but to *touch* him.

It is this additional demand of Thomas that gives us the decisive clue to his character. He is a doubter. Yes. But more, he is a stubborn, obstinate, practical-minded, proof-oriented person, determined in his demand for a revelation that exceeded even what the other disciples had experienced.

Belief Made Difficult

This, then, is the first lesson of our text: *Thomas made belief in the risen Lord difficult for himself by his demands.*

Once we face the fact that it was Thomas himself who

made faith difficult by his unreasonable demands, we can understand the extent to which our Lord was willing to go to convince Thomas and bring him to belief.

A week later, according to John, the disciples were again together. This time Thomas was with them. Again Jesus appeared and stood among them. "Peace be with you," he said, and then turning to Thomas and pointing to the wounds in his body, he said, "Put your finger here, and look at my hands. Then stretch out your hand and put it in my side." Jesus used the exact words Thomas had expressed in his demands.

Jesus Condescends

These words and this action of our Lord directed to Thomas brings us to the second lesson of our text: *Christ did not think Thomas' demands were too difficult to meet and defeat.* Jesus willingly condescended to Thomas' unwarranted demands. Jesus acquiesced to the demands of Thomas as a slave obeying his master. Our Lord did what he had done so often before; Jesus the master assumed the role of a servant.

To see the risen Lord was not enough for Thomas. He had to *touch.* Privileged with the opportunity of being one of the few people of history to see the holy and risen Lord, Thomas demanded to touch the Lord in order to believe. Yet, wonder of wonders, Christ did not chide or rebuke Thomas' insolence — he yielded to it. Jesus, the victorious Lord of both life and death, he who was with the Father when the earth was created and the moon and the stars were hung in the heavens; he who was present when all that exists was formed and fashioned; this God among men, bowed and humbled himself, submitted himself to the stubborn demands of a mere mortal. The exulted Lord lowered himself to the level of Thomas' self-centered stubbornness. So astonishing and amazing is this sensational, inconceivable act of our Lord's accommodation to Thomas that we should designate this event by establishing a festival of our Lord's *condescension.* The Resurrection was our Lord's victory over death and the grave. The Ascension was our Lord's victory over time and space. But this act of condescension before Thomas was our Lord's victory over human doubts and demands.

Is it any wonder, then, that Thomas, confronted by such a love-bent, caring, condescending Lord, broke and fell before his master, crying out, "My Lord and my God"? Thomas knew that he did not deserve such treatment. He knew that only God, who is pure love, could be so bold as to bow before such blatant disrespect. Thomas knew that he stood in the presence of more than a man; he was experiencing God present among us.

It is not surprising that Thomas never followed through with his demands even when the opportunity was given him. He never touched the Lord, because Christ had touched him at his most vulnerable spot. Christ touched Thomas at the point of his strength — his pride. Thomas exposed the focus of his life — himself and his demands. By laying down the requirements by which he would believe, he had laid himself open to a Lord who was willing to meet all his demands, no matter how unreasonable, because Christ loved Thomas more than Thomas loved himself. Christ picked up Thomas' challenge and thrust it back upon him so that it was Thomas who had to back away from his own demands. Thomas realized to his utter shame how unjust and wrong his demands were. Thomas knew he had created, by his own doubts and demands, a barricade between himself and his God. Thomas was literally defeated by his own demands. That is why Thomas stands before us in our text, not only as a *defeated doubter,* but as an example of the self-damnation we impose upon ourselves when we make belief in the risen Lord dependent upon our own unreasonable demands.

We are our own worst enemies. We judge ourselves by our own pride, hard-heartedness, little-mindedness when we stand before the Lord who is so willing to go to any lengths to conquer us and win us to belief in him. This is truly to discover justification by faith the hard way. This is the gospel of our Lord's willingness to humble himself, not only on the cross, but beyond the cross, to bring us before our creator God as willing believers.

We are so often tempted to think that believing would be so much easier if we could only see and touch Jesus. But the truth revealed to us through Thomas is that this is the *hard way* to faith and belief. Thomas created his own difficult way to belief by his demands to see and touch the Lord. He paid the price of utter shame before the loving kindness and condescension of God. Undoubtedly, Thomas regretted all his life that he had forced his Lord to so humble himself. How much easier it would have been if only Thomas had accepted the word and testimony of his companions — how much easier for the Lord and how much easier for Thomas.

First then, Thomas made belief difficult for himself by his demands. Second, Christ did not find Thomas' demands too difficult to meet and defeat. Which brings us to the third lesson of our text: *Jesus says to us that there is a better way to belief.*

A Better Way

Christ tells us in our text that there is a better and easier way to belief than Thomas followed. Christ says, "Blessed are those who believe without (the demands of) seeing me." Or perhaps more to the point, Christ is saying to us that the better way to belief is to make no demands — lay down no ultimatums — place no requirements on our act of belief, but accept belief in Christ as the risen Lord as a *gift* of the word.

The word is God's gift to us that we might believe. There are no demands placed on a gift. A gift is given as a complete surprise. To place requirements on our acceptance of a gift is to destroy the whole act of giving. The heart of the Gospel is not only good news but a *new goodness* that is given rather than earned. God gives belief as he gives himself, freely, without requirements or demands either on his part as giver or on our part as receiver. Belief is an act of love. As God places no demands on our receiving the gift, so we are to place no demands on our accepting of it. Belief is a free, spontaneous response of one lover to another. To place demands on God's gift is to create for ourselves difficulties to belief that are not only unnecessary but insulting to God's gracious giving.

The story of Thomas assures us that God is not afraid of our doubts; he is most willing to deal with our unreasonable demands. But the story of Thomas tells us so much more. It proclaims there is a better way to belief than through doubts and demands, and that better way is the way of *hearing* and *believing*. It is the way of the gracious receiver. It is the way of the child who trusts his loving parents and knows that whatever the parent says is true, because it is a word spoken *in* love and *from* love and *to* love.

Thomas created for himself the difficult way to belief. He fought the hard fight of faith through doubts and demands, and God brought him through the ordeal. God will do the same for us; but God says to us that it is not necessary to pass through the crucible of doubt and demands as Thomas did. There is an easier way and a better way — the way of simple trust in the word of God.

A Better Crossing

During the early days of our country a young soldier was separated from his company and was attempting to make his way back to the safety of the fort. There was no path to follow in this wilderness. Only the slowly setting sun gave him the general direction he should travel.

Suddenly out of nowhere, an Indian scout appeared alongside of him. He was not certain whether to trust him or not. But in this wild and dangerous territory, he was glad for the companionship of even a doubtful friend.

As they rode toward the fort, they came to a river swollen by the recent rains. The water was wild and swift, filled with jagged rock and slippery boulders. The young soldier knew that the fort was directly ahead across the rapids. The Indian pointed to a curve in the river. "Down there beyond the bend," he said, "the river is wide and shallow. Much better for crossing."

The young soldier looked down the river. It was quite a distance to the bend, and he was not sure what possible dangers might lie in wait for him along the wooded banks on this hostile side of the river.

"No," said the young man, "I'll go my own way — the way I can see — straight across." The Indian left him and went on down stream toward the bend in the river.

The young soldier plunged into the river. The current struck him with stupendous force, knocking him from his horse. Frantically, he fought the raging current. He was thrown against a boulder. His arm snapped, and the jagged rocks cut into his legs and sides. He clutched to a rock. Regaining his strength, he struggled against the brutal current and painfully made his way from one rock to another until he reached the other side of the river and crawled out onto the muddy bank exhausted, cut and bruised with his broken arm throbbing with pain.

From this vantage point he could look down the stream, beyond the bend in the river. As the scout had said, the river was wide and calm. He watched as the old Indian easily and comfortably rode his horse across the shallow waters.

So with us. There are many ways to come to faith and

belief. We can listen and trust in the experience of others, or we can forge our own way through doubts and demands as Thomas did. But our Lord says in our text that there is a better way. It is the way that makes no demands of God. It is the way of the gift of God's word. It is the way of the humble, the obedient, those who simply listen to the word of God, trust the word and take God at his word. This is the better way to belief, a way where the river of faith is wide and calm and shallow. Our Lord calls us to this way, saying, "Blessed are those who take the easy way, making no demands, but simply trusting God and thereby believe without seeing."

With the Wings of Eagles

THIRD SUNDAY OF EASTER
Luke 24:13-35

Have you ever felt that you just had to get away from it all? Well-prepared plans fall to pieces, an important deal dissolves, someone you trusted lets you down, a marriage made in heaven is slowly becoming a living hell. Life comes apart at the seams, or just things in general build up pressure and you know you have to get away from it all.

Well, if you have ever felt like that, then you can appreciate the condition of our two men in the Gospel lesson for this morning.

It was Sunday afternoon. Friday, Jesus had died. They had gone up to Calvary to be with their leader in his final tragic moments on earth, or so they thought. The next day was Saturday, their Holy Day, like our Sunday. Undoubtedly it was a low day, like the day after someone we love dies.

On the day of the funeral, friends and relatives gather round us. There is activity. People are trying their best to comfort us, make small talk, be polite and thoughtful. Food is brought in by the neighbors. Our minds are in limbo as we eat and are not really hungry; talk, and really don't know what we are saying, or really care.

Then comes the day after the funeral. It is quiet. Most people are gone, and we are left alone to deal for the first time with our loneliness and our loss. That's when we think, "I'd like to get away from it all."

When our text opens, it is Sunday — two days after our Lord's death on the cross. Since Saturday is the Jewish Sabbath, Sunday for the apostles would be like our Monday, the day when we go back to work. For the followers of Jesus, it meant going back to their fishing nets and boats, their barnyards and vineyards, their flocks and grassy fields — back to whatever they left behind when they took up with this man called Jesus.

The text says that the two men were on the road to Emmaus. It was a no-place kind of a town. A village where nothing important ever happened. But that didn't matter. All that mattered was that it was away from Jerusalem, and they wanted to escape Jerusalem, turn their backs upon it, get away from it all — the arrest, the trial, the cross, the cruel death.

This was a normal reaction. We all do it. When things go bad, turn sour, fall through, we head out for Emmaus. We don't care where it is so long as it is far away from where we have been. Our road to Emmaus may be the corner bar or the lake or the mountains or if we can afford it, a trip across the country or a jet ride to Europe. Nowhere in particular, as long as it is somewhere away from where we are.

It was here on the road to Emmaus that Jesus came to these two men. It is on our roads to Emmaus that he is most likely to come to us. Wherever we go to escape life is exactly where we should expect to be confronted by our Lord. For he is the Lord of life, and whenever we give up on life and try to call it quits, he comes calling us and drawing us back to life. That's the one thing we can expect when we try to escape life: Our Lord won't let us, because he gave up his life that we might not give up on ours. He lived and died that our life might be saved, not extended, but changed; transformed into an abundant life, a new life, a resurrected life, a life that we do not want to run away from, but run to. A life that means every morning when we get up, we are glad to be alive, not simply living but excited about really being alive. A life that takes us to the window every morning, saying, "Good morning, God!" not "Good god, it's morning!"

When Jesus comes to give us this new and transformed life, he will more than likely come as he came to these two men on the road to Emmaus. He will come as a friend who walks beside us. He will not come as a spiritual vision, a god-like creature glowing with an unearthly light, or with a heavenly halo neatly hovering above his head. He will not come as one from outer space — a glorified E.T., but as an old and cherished friend. He will talk with us and even stay with us to share an evening supper.

So we have a real stake in what happened that certain Sunday on an uncertain road to Emmaus, because these men are where we so often are, and our Lord comes to us as he came to them. It is important, therefore, that we understand, in so far as possible, what actually happened in our text for this morning. To do that, we have to move back in the story about three years to the time when these two men of our Gospel lesson had their *faces* and *not* their *backs* turned toward Jerusalem.

They were embarking on an exciting adventure with a man called Jesus. He was a nobody from a country village, the son of a carpenter, but when he spoke, it was as if God himself were present and speaking to his people. It wasn't long before they enthusiastically supported him as a new Messiah. They hailed him as a hero, the harbinger of all their hopes. But before they really got to know him, he was dead, and so were all their dreams for a new world and a new life. "The New Messiah Movement" came to a sudden halt just outside the walls of Jerusalem on a hill above a garbage dump called Golgotha. It was so close to the Holy City but so far away from a new and better world. At the foot of the cross their road to glory came to a bitter and decisive dead-end. So they turned tail and turned their backs on Jerusalem.

They had gambled all and lost. It was a total wipe out! But what an adventure, what an experience it had been while it lasted. They had cheered triumphantly with the crowds as Jesus entered Jerusalem on that first Palm Sunday. They had watched admiringly as their leader took a whip and drove the money changers out of the temple. They were dumbfounded when they heard Judas had betrayed their master and Peter had denied him. They were distressed and uneasy when they saw their beloved teacher stand trial before Pilate. They hovered in fear among the angry mob when he was crucified as a common criminal on Calvary. They had grieved with the other disciples when Jesus lay alone and forsaken in the tomb. They had even been present when the flustered women ran breathless from the garden grave, reporting the fantastic fact that the tomb of their Lord was empty. In their own words, they had hoped through all these adventurous and often anxious moments that he was the *one* to redeem Israel. But for them, Easter morning came and no light broke forth from the horizon. No army of angels came to avenge the killing of their Lord. They saw only dark clouds of doubt, despair, perhaps even personal disaster for themselves. Therefore, fearing for their own safety, they had turned their backs on Jerusalem and were headed toward Emmaus, the no-place-in-particular city.

Think of it, these two men — one named Cleopas and the other man unnamed — had seen, had heard, had hoped, and still had not believed. The well-loved Spiritual asks the question, "Were you there when they crucified my Lord?" implying that if we had been there, we would surely believe. These two men had been there. They had seen it all, hoped it all hundreds of times in their hearts, but still they *did not believe!*

What chance, then, is there for us who are separated from the events of redemption by two thousand years? If these two men were there, seeing, hearing, hoping, and were still not brought to belief, how can we ever expect to believe in the resurrection of our Christ?

The answer to this very direct question of how we can have faith, is in our lesson read this morning. But it can be easily overlooked if we miss the clue given us by the writers of the first and second lessons. Our first lesson from the book of Acts ends with the phrase, "Jesus — God raised up." In the second lesson the author of First Peter states, "God raised him from the dead." Both of these passages of Scripture stress that the resurrection — our Lord's emerging from the tomb and his victory over death — was an *act of God.* It was God the Father who raised Jesus from the dead.

Sometimes the resurrection is presented as an inevitable event resulting from the fact that Jesus was divine and therefore could not really die, at least not stay dead. It is sort of a you-can't-keep-a-good-man-down kind of theology. After all, you can't kill God and bury him and expect him to stay dead and buried!

There is some truth in such an interpretation of the resurrection event. Jesus was divine. Jesus was God, and he could have exercised his divine power at any time he wanted to and put a stop to the atrocious affair. He could have called forth an army of angels and slain King Pilate and his whole royal court on the spot if he had wanted to. He could have thrown thunderbolts of lightning and burned the Scribes and Pharisees to cinders if he had wanted to. With a single blow, he could have eliminated the vast armies of Rome and knocked mighty Caesar from his throne if he had wanted to, but *he didn't.*

Our Lord was submissive and quiet, non-violent and meek. He did not resist nor did he summon forth his potential power. No! Just the opposite. He surrendered. He struggled under the heavy load of the cross and suffered the pain of the nails, the mockery of spit streaming down his face, the agony of hanging naked in the sweltering heat of a noon-day sun. And he died! He denied this earthly life and chose death, willingly, willfully. Because in the mysterious mind-set he shared with God his Father, he knew that this life, which we so highly prize, is tentative, tenuous and temporary.

This life we cling to, as if there is nothing else, can be lost in a flashing second by disease or accident. A speeding car out of control, a flying bullet hitting its mark, a stroke striking us down, or just the silent passage of time taking its toll, and life is snatched from us. We have nothing, nothing but a cold, factual grave-marker driven into the dirt in which we lie and in which we dissolve into the dust from whence we came. Ashes to ashes, dust to dust is all there is. But not so for Jesus Christ.

Our Lord knew that this life is not all there is. There is more, much more; a greater life than we have ever known. Our Lord knew that it was the work and will of God the Father to give to his chosen children a new life. Jesus our Lord knew God intended us for a higher destiny — not a life limited from dust to dust, but a divine destiny, a life lived in continual fellowship and communion with him who had created us, our Father God. Our Lord knew that the way to this new life, this eternal life, was through his humiliation and death. For there can be no resurrection life except through death.

As God the Father gave life at the beginning of creation, so it is God the Father who gives life on the cross and from the cross, in the tomb and by the tomb. That is why our first and second lessons both declare it is *God* who raised Jesus from the dead and it is God who gives him the new life of glory.

So with us. We can never gain life, earn it by our own merit, attain it by our own goodness, claim it because of some spiritual soul within us. This new life is a gift, a gift from God. There is nothing we can do to believe or accept it, by ourselves or on our own. Even if we could be with these two men on their way to Emmaus and walk and talk with Jesus; even if we could have walked in their shoes and experienced for ourselves the triumphant entry, the trial, the cross; even if we could have heard with our own ears the witness of those women on that first Easter morning, "He is risen" — still we could not believe unless God gives us the gift, the gift of the new and resurrected life.

The two men in our Gospel had not only been present through all the history-shaking events of redemption: they were actually walking and talking with the risen Lord, and still they did not believe. It was only when Jesus directed them to what God had spoken in the Scriptures; it was only when Jesus sat with them at their supper table and broke bread with them and thereby became the instrument, the means by which God touched them and enlivened them and opened their eyes and hearts, that these men could believe.

You see, it is not enough that Jesus went to the cross and died for us. It is not enough that he rose from the grave for us. No! Nothing done *for* us is enough; something must happen *in* us and *to* us. As God opened the tomb that first Easter morn and raised Jesus from the dead, so God must open the tomb in which we are buried and raise us to a new life. For the new life is not something gained from first-hand knowledge or from direct involvement or even participation. It is a *gift*, a gift given to us and placed *in us* by God and God alone.

Christ was obedient. Christ was obedient even unto death; but his glory was not earned or gained; it was given. It was an act of God, an act of grace, and to share in the glory of new life, we too must be given that life by God. Something must happen not only *for* us, but *in* us.

These two men walking on the road to Emmaus said to each other, "Did not our hearts burn *within* us while he talked to us and opened to us the scriptures." They were testifying to the fact that God was at work in them. They were in a tomb, buried by defeat and death. What they needed was not to witness a resurrection but to experience a resurrection within themselves.

Norman Vincent Peale tells of sharing a crowded taxi on the way to preaching a sermon at a large conference. The taxi driver was complaining about all his problems and troubles. He was convinced that the whole world was filled with crooks, and everything and everybody was rapidly going to hell.

"Tell 'em that at your rally, reverend," the cab driver said.

Beside Dr. Peale there was a heavy-set, jolly lady with a big happy face. She leaned over to Dr. Peale and said, "Don't do it. We all know that. Tell them instead about Jesus and how he came to give us all God's gift of a resurrected life."

Then the lady reached over and tapped the taxi driver on the shoulder, saying, "Young man — what you need is to get resurrected."

That is precisely what we all need. It isn't enough just to see and hear and hope in a resurrection done for us; we need something to happen in us. We need to get resurrected!

The decisive question then is "how?" How can we get God to work a resurrection in us? How do we convince God to open our eyes and our hearts so that we can truly believe in the resurrected Lord and share with him the new resurrected life?

The agonizing answer is — we *cannot!* There is nothing we can do to earn or gain or merit a resurrection, because all resurrections are a gift. God gave victory and life and glory to Christ; it is only God who can give a resurrected life to us. But above the agonizing answer that we can do nothing is the gospel, the glorious good news that what we cannot gain for ourselves, God willingly gives to us as a gift now.

We are not like the men on the road to Emmaus with our backs turned toward Jerusalem, meeting Christ as a stranger. We are a people facing Jerusalem. We have been converted, changed, turned about, which is what conversion means. This has happened in our *baptism.* God has given us the gift of the new and resurrected life at the *font.*

The baptismal font is our Jerusalem where we experience the cross of Calvary and the open tomb of the garden. The baptismal font is our road to Emmaus where Christ comes to us not as a stranger but as a *Savior* bringing to us a gift of new life from God the Father. It is planted within us as a seed, a seed of light that burns within us and opens our ears to the meaning of Scripture and opens our eyes to see the Lord who is present and presides over the supper table of his holy communion.

We do not need another Pentecost or a second baptism or the experience of being twice-born. Jerusalem, Calvary, Pentecost, second birth, new life are within us. As we were baptized, we have already received the new and resurrected life. Our only responsibility is to relax, surrender, hang loose and let the new life live and grow within us.

God has not forsaken us. Through word and sacrament he feeds and nourishes the seed of new life he has given us, and he will never leave us until that new life flourishes to its full maturity and we know the full glory of this gift of grace and rise with Christ into the new world which is to come.

While climbing a cliff one day, two little boys found a nest of eagle's eggs. They put the eggs under a hen in the barnyard and in due time, the young eaglets hatched with the chicks. The mother hen cared for them as though they were her own.

One day after the eaglets had grown, a great eagle swooped down over the barnyard and something stirred within the young eagles. Day after day the great eagle came. Day after day something stirred within the young eagles, and their wings felt the birth of potential strength within them.

Then one day when the great eagle came and swooped down over the barnyard, the young eagles dared — they flapped their wings and flew. Their destiny to be eagles, born within them would not be denied. They were born to fly!

So with us. Most of our days we live in a barnyard we call our world, knowing all the while there is more, because, though we are in a barnyard, we are not of it. By our baptism, we were born from above.

We may live like chickens — even sometimes look like chickens, but we were born at the font to be eagles. Every now and then when we are engaged in public worship or in the private closet of our personal devotions, when we are reading the Scriptures or participating in the sacraments or sharing our faith with fellow believers, the eagle of God's spirit swoops down from heaven and something stirs within us. Our hearts burn within us, and we know that this barnyard is not all there is. There is more. We know that one day our new life will stretch its wings, lift us from this barnyard, and we will soar above the suffering and sorrows of this sordid existence and experience the freedom of the full new life God has given us in our baptism.

As early as the Book of Exodus, God promised us through Moses (19:4), "I will bare you on eagles wings and bring you unto myself." And by the prophet Isaiah God confirmed this promise (40:31),

They that wait upon the Lord
shall renew their strength;
they shall mount up with wings as eagles;
they shall run and not be weary
and they shall walk and not faint.

In Jesus Christ God's promise is fulfilled. By our baptism into Christ the promise becomes a gift given. We are a resurrected people. As Christ is risen, so shall we rise to a new life. Our face has been turned to Jerusalem, and truly we shall rise up with wings as eagles — and fly!

The Door to Life

FOURTH SUNDAY OF EASTER
John 10:1-10

One of the most appealing designations of our Lord in church literature, hymns and art is Jesus as the Good Shepherd.

In our Gospel lesson this morning, Jesus refers to himself as the "shepherd of the sheep," and in the verse that immediately follows our text, Jesus calls himself the "Good Shepherd."

The truth is, however, Jesus was not a shepherd. There is no record in the New Testament or in all the tradition that surrounds it that he ever kept sheep. He was a carpenter by trade and the son of a carpenter. He lived most of his life in sheep-raising country, and must have seen and known many shepherds, but he himself was never a shepherd. Which means that we are dealing here in this text with a symbol — a symbol of leadership. As a shepherd leads his sheep, so Christ is the one who leads.

The second truth is that "good" is not the best translation of John's record of what Jesus said. When we use the word "good" in our daily conversation, we think in terms of the ethical or moral character of a person. Good children mind their parents and never get into trouble. A good person is clean and decent, never breaking any of the accepted rules either of religion or society.

When John uses the Greek word *kalos,* it means much more than a moral characteristic of the personality.

It means "noble," or "model." It means the "ideal," the "true," the "real." Therefore, when John says that Jesus spoke of himself as the "good shepherd," he understands our Lord to be presenting himself as a model — an example of true leadership.

To introduce his claim that he is the Good Shepherd, our Lord tells the *Parable of the Sheepfold.* You will not find this story included in most books that cover the parables. It may be that the image of the Good Shepherd is so strong that it dominates this first section of John's tenth chapter, and the parable is thereby overlooked. Or it may be that the parable is too difficult to interpret. John seems to indicate this, for he records that, when Jesus first told the parable, the disciples failed to understand its meaning. It would follow that if the disciples, who lived in a sheep-raising country and saw shepherds every day, failed to understand it, what hope is there for us who see sheep so seldom and more than likely have never known a shepherd? The Parable of the Sheepfold with sheep going in and out of its gate doesn't carry much meaning to twentieth century Christians.

In the text, when Jesus realizes that the disciples do not understand what he is saying, he changes his metaphor, his image, to a more familiar one. He says, "I am the door." This is a more universal image.

We all see and use doors everyday. They are the way we go in and out of our homes and offices, our stores and factories. For the most part, we take doors for granted without even thinking about them. But nothing is perhaps more frustrating than a blocked or a locked door when we want to go into, or get out of some place.

If we are outside our home and have forgotten or lost our house key, a locked door is really no door at all. We frantically attempt to find another way in.

If we are inside a room or a building and something happens like a fire, and we try to escape, finding the doors blocked or locked is nothing short of panic.

So doors are important. This is particularly true in our text, for the door Jesus is talking about is the door, the passage, the way, the means of getting into the Kingdom of God. That is a vital door for all of us who are seekers after salvation.

In the ninth chapter of John, Jesus healed the young man born blind, and we saw the great difficulty this miracle of healing caused the young man. His parents wouldn't accept it because they were afraid of the Jewish leaders who had agreed that if anyone professed that Jesus was the Messiah, they would be put out of the synagogue.

The Jewish leaders wouldn't accept the miracle because they could not conceive of a man sent from God healing on the Sabbath. So far as they were concerned, Jesus was not a prophet, a miracle worker, or a leader at all, but a sinner.

Jesus' response to the Pharisees was not gentle. He pointed out that it was really the Pharisees who were blind, and if not blind, then certainly guilty before God for failing to recognize and accept him as a true prophet and leader sent from God.

So the *Parables of the Sheepfold* and the *Door* were told not only for the understanding of the disciples and for the instruction of us who desire salvation, but they were told to attack the misunderstanding of the Pharisees.

Jesus uses the image of the Good Shepherd and the Door as symbols or examples of his leadership. What he is basically saying in both of these images is that *good leaders don't climb walls; they create doors.*

Now what did he mean by that? Jesus is teaching by using *contrast.* Our Lord is comparing his leadership with that of those who claim to be the true leaders of the Jewish people. Bad leaders, Jesus graphically points out, *climb walls,* whereas good leaders *create doors.*

To emphasize this, our Lord uses some very strong

language. Referring to the bad leaders, our Lord says: "All others who came before me are thieves and robbers."

Scholars, such as Alan Richardson in the Torch Commentary, point out that the first time Jesus uses the phrase, "thieves and robbers" (10:1), he is referring to the "sheep-stealers" who preyed upon congregations in big cities — schismatics, heretics, false Messiahs, etc.

The second time our Lord uses the phrase, "thieves and robbers" (10:8), he is referring to the rulers who fatten themselves at the expense of the flock, the Sadducean high priests and Pharisaic doctors of the law and the politicans like Herod and the Roman procurators.

In both cases, he is referring to people in positions of power and leadership who should have been concerned for their followers but were not; instead they were concerned only for themselves.

You see, leaders who climb walls are thieves and robbers, not because they choose the easy way. No. It is often more difficult to climb over walls than to go through the gate or a door. The reason these leaders were false is that they managed to get in where they wanted to be, but they provided no way for others to follow after them.

Sheep who follow shepherds cannot climb walls; they can only go in by the gate. Therefore, leaders who climb walls are robbers because they think only of themselves and provide no way for their followers to come after them. In the case of the Pharisees, their expert knowledge of the law and their expansion of the law made it impossible for anyone except professionals like themselves to follow the law. They made righteousness so difficult that average persons were defeated in their attempts to obey the law before they ever started.

The Pharisees actually created walls and barriers and then prided themselves on their ability to climb over them. The Pharisees were great climbers. Jesus, however, challenged their wall-climbing and declared to them that *good leaders don't climb walls, they create doors.*

Perhaps a modern parable would help at this point. The following story appeared in a California newspaper during one of the forest fires that so frequently destroy vast areas of western timberlands.

Harvey was a Boy Scout leader. He had twelve boys with him on a camping trip in the hills of California. One morning when they woke, they smelled smoke. The wind suddenly changed and there was no doubt about it as smoke came rolling into the camp site — the forest was on fire.

Quickly they gathered up their gear and headed for the nearby river. When they arrived at the river bank, Harvey said, "We'll swim across and once we are on the other side we will be safe."

Most of the boys instantly pulled off their boots and jumped into the stream. But four of the troop stood motionless with fear flooding their faces.

"What's the matter with you?" shouted Harvey. "The fire is right behind us — jump in!"

The four boys screamed in chorus, "We can't swim!"

For a moment Harvey panicked. He knew that he didn't have time to carry each boy across the river and return for the others. Then an idea came to him. He took a rope hanging from his back-pack and tied it to a tree on the river bank. Then he said, "I'm going to swim across the river to the other side and tie this rope to a tree. The rope will be just a few inches above the water. Jump in the river — hold on to the rope and pull yourselves across."

Harvey swam the river, secured the rope, and the four boys pulled themselves to safety.

Now this is what our Lord is talking about. Leaders who think only of their own safety are false leaders. They are thieves and robbers of others' lives. They literally rob their followers of life by failing to provide a way for them.

True leaders, good shepherds, model leaders, think first of their followers. They find a way not for themselves alone, but their first concern is placed on those for whom they are responsible.

True leaders not only discover a way, they make a way. They create doors and bridges that others might follow after them. A brilliant and courageous person may pioneer an uncharted wilderness, sail an unknown sea, discover a new land; but a true leader is a map-maker, a bridge-builder, a road-maker, a trail-blazer. A true leader is not in it for the thrill of adventure or the glamour of conquest. A true leader is one who makes a way for others. *Good leaders don't climb walls, they create doors.*

It was a single deed of daring when God became man, took on human flesh and tabernacled among us. It was a dangerous drama of devotion when Jesus ate with sinners. It was a comprehensive conquest of compassion when the Son of God healed on the Sabbath. It was an unparalleled act of sacrifice when Christ the Messiah went innocently to a criminal's cross and suffered the indignities of a painful death. Wonder of wonders, he did all this, not for himself, but totally and completely for others, for us!

The Pharisees were good and righteous men. They worked hard at achieving their salutary status of moral leadership among people. No honest observer can fault the Pharisees for their efforts. But as leaders of the people, they were thieves and robbers because they were climbers, wall climbers and not door builders. They displayed publicly the accomplished goal of the fulfilled law. They were sterling examples of self-achieved righteousness. But instead of helping others find a way to righteousness, they stood by and judged others because they could not measure up to their perfected performances of piety. Jesus said, "Such leaders are thieves and robbers." *Good leaders don't climb walls, they create doors.*

Are we not often guilty of the same thing, particularly in the church? We use God's teachings to our own advantage. We delight in pointing out the faults of others and thereby focus the spotlight on our own virtues. The demonic aspect of such attitudes and actions is that we carefully pick and choose those teachings of our Lord that best fit our own capabilities and circumstances.

This is not just limited to the church. So often our total lifestyle is to build walls around our *own* way of living or our own beliefs and then look down from the top of these walls at others who are struggling to make it in our competitive world. How easy it is for us, the saved and the successful, to slander the sinners and failures. The drunkard is weak. The unemployed is lazy. The common laborers are uneducated. The criminal element is beyond reform. Anyone who doesn't think and act like we do is a communist, a red neck, or a pervert — or to put it more politely, "socially undesirable." We use our talents and abilities and blessings not to become leaders who help others but to become celebrities — apart from others, above others, better than others, admired and respected by others. Such selfish, ego-centric motives betray us for what we are, not good shepherds and true leaders, but thieves and robbers.

In the midst of our cheap and shoddy lives, in the face of all this misused and misguided leadership, this profitless use of power, skill, and talent, Christ comes to us and speaks to us as he spoke to the disciples, pointing to himself as both the model of true leadership and the door to a new way of living.

True, we cannot measure up to the example of leadership which he exhibits, but we can put aside our false pretentions and acknowledge that he and he alone is leader. We can throw ourselves on his mercy and trust him to make of us the type of leaders within our church and community that he desires us to be. We can let his spirit of self-sacrifice and self-giving enter into our lives and reform us to his design.

The Pharisees failed because they refused to change. They saw the temple fall and the Holy City of Jerusalem in ashes under their leadership. They who condemned thieves and robbers and sinners *became* the greatest of thieves and robbers and sinners, and they are remembered only as those who opposed our Lord and denied his Messiahship.

Thank God there is still time for us to change. Thank God the door to the sheepfold is still open. Thank God that he willingly grants us this day of grace wherein we can acknowledge the leadership of Christ and bow before him as Lord and King.

Christ takes no delight in putting us down. But our Lord knows that the only hope for abundant life, here-and-now in the hereafter is by way of the destruction of our pride, the forsaking of our false gods, and the humiliation of our own human ambitions. It is not easy to follow once we have known the personal elation and satisfaction of being in positions of power and leadership; but refusing to follow the Good Shepherd is sheer folly, for he is the only door. He alone can give us life.

A professor was touring the Holy Land with a bus load of students. One day he was lecturing on the text of the Good Shepherd, and he pointed out that in Palestine the shepherds lead the sheep rather than going behind them and driving them as they do in most other parts of the world.

Just as he was emphatically making this point, the bus stopped to let a flock of sheep cross the road. To everyone's surprise, there was a man with a whip, driving them from behind.

The students snickered and looked questioningly at their professor. Obviously disturbed and embarrassed, the professor jumped from the bus and called out to the man driving the sheep, "My friend, I have always been told that shepherds in Palestine lead their sheep. They do not drive them as you are doing."

The old man driving the sheep with a whip called back, "You are absolutely right; but you see, I am not the shepherd — I am the village butcher."

Christ stands before us today as the model example of all true leadership. He is the Good Shepherd. That image has something to say to all of us — both as leaders and followers. Christ alone is the door. He alone possesses the right way, the only way to abundant living. Therefore, look to the Lord, Jesus the Christ, for he and he alone is the standard by which all leadership, including our own efforts to lead others, can be evaluated. He alone enables us to know the difference between a shepherd and a butcher.

Christ is the model leader. Christ is the Good Shepherd. Christ is the Door. Thank God, the door is still open.

Space in the Heart of God

FIFTH SUNDAY OF EASTER
John 14:1-12

We frequently hear people begin a conversation with the statement: "I have some good news for you and some bad."

This phrase describes the situation in which the disciples find themselves in our Gospel lesson for today. Before our lesson opens, Jesus had just told the disciples the bad news. He has hit them right between the eyes with three knock-out blows.

First Blow: Betrayal

With the first blow, our Lord bewildered the disciples with the blunt statement: "One of you is going to betray me." He then takes a piece of bread and dips it into a pan of gravy and gives it to Judas. As soon as Judas received the bread, he left the table and went out into the night Apparently, the disciples did not make the connection and thought that Judas was leaving to pay some bills. The thought of one of their own betraying the Lord still bothered and bewildered them.

Second Blow: Denial

After Judas had left the room, Jesus turned to Peter. There was a short exchange of words, and then the second blow. Jesus said to Peter, "Before the cock crows you will deny me three times." That was a shocker. Peter was highly respected in the fellowship and was actually second in command to the Lord himself. Denial? They could not believe their ears.

Third Blow: Departure

Betrayal! Denial! That was a heavy load to lay upon the disciples; but the thing that really broke their spirits was the announcement by the Lord that he was going away. Betrayal, they didn't understand. Denial, they found hard to believe; but the departure of their leader and Lord was a devastating blow — a disaster — a knock-out blow.

We can sympathize with the frustration of the disciples, for this is where many of us find ourselves today. We struggle to survive in a world of bad news. On the world front, wars break out in South Africa, South America and the Middle East. Riots rage in Poland and Northern Ireland. Nuclear arms build-up spreads from the greater nations to the smaller ones. On the home front, taxes and inflation race with unemployment to dominate the headlines. Everything we do causes cancer, and our best friend drops dead from a heart attack. Panic! Nothing gets better; everything gets worse. Frustration ties our minds into knots, flooding our imagination with hideous images of even more horrible disasters ahead. Fear grabs hold of our hearts with cold and clammy hands, and we cry out in our despair, "Where are you, Lord, when we need you most?"

The Good News

In our Gospel lesson, Christ gives us an answer as he speaks to the disciples. He tells them the good news. "Let not your hearts be troubled," says the Lord. "Believe in God, believe also in me." By these words he is declaring that he is departing from his disciples, but he is not *deserting them.* That is a big difference.

These words were difficult for the disciples to understand; they are difficult for us, as difficult as it is when we try to convince our children when we leave for work that we are not deserting them or running away from them, but doing what is necessary to earn a salary that puts food in their mouths, a shelter over their heads, and gives them as much of the good things in life as possible.

Despite the passing years, we never quite outgrew this fear of being left alone in a hostile world — so with children, so with the disciples, so with us. The remedy our Lord offers to this nauseous feeling of being alone is simple, believe in God and believe in me.

Here Jesus is saying that the Father God and he are one. There is so much theology tucked into this concept that we would exhaust all the books of the Bible in any attempt to fathom the depth of its meaning. Yet the intent of our Lord in making this profound claim is simple and direct. He and the Father are one in their total and complete concern and love for each one of us.

The disciples had a strong background of belief in God supported by generations of evidence that God cared and was especially concerned for them. God had delivered them as a people from bondage and slavery in Egypt. He had sent prophets with words burning on their lips as they proclaimed the faithfulness of God. They were assured again and again of the Father's divine determination to be their God and loving Father.

To all this sacred history Jesus adds his simple story. He had taught the disciples in parables and acted out in miracles the Father's love alive in him. He had pointed out that when they were weak and forgot God, God did not forget them. When they were rebellious and turned away from God, he never turned his face from them. When they asked for bread, God did not give them a stone. Jesus said and did everything to bring constantly into their remembrance that they were God's chosen children. Now he is calling the disciples to appropriate in their lives the historic love of God for them by trusting in the faithful father. Trust the Father. Trust me, for we are one in our love for you.

This is the key to our Gospel this morning and to the whole gospel within the Scriptures. This is the good news that overcomes all the bad news. This is the light in the darkness. This is the good news that gives security and stability and strength to us in the most troubled of times.

Many Mansions

Having pointed out the unity between himself and the Father, Jesus then adds, "In my father's house there are many mansions." These are familiar words. We have heard them many times at funerals and when our home has been left empty by the death of a loved one. They are comforting words. But they continue to confound the scholars and interpreters of the Bible. Any time you start talking about heaven, you are on controversial ground, because words like death, everlasting life, and heaven are filled with emotional involvement.

Fundamentalists take these words quite literally. Heaven is a *place* — a city in the sky with high-rise condominiums and streets paved with gold. Other elaborations are added by tradition, pearly gates, angel wings, halos and harps. Our imaginations are challenged by this baggage of centuries of wondering, wishing, and hoping. It is what we want to believe. We may listen to the fundamentalists with a superior sense of sophistication but many of us secretly wish it were so.

The liberals interpret these words of Jesus about mansions in the sky by and by, symbolically, declaring that heaven is not a place but a *condition*. Heaven is a spiritual relationship between God and us. Heaven is not some place we go after we die; it is a condition of life now. It is a condition built into the very structure of our cause-and-effect world. Do good deeds, and they will bring about their own rewards. Do wrong and you will suffer the consequences. It is just as natural as night following day. This built-in judgment of life is not very satisfying or comforting when we stand by an open grave and see our loved one lowered into an empty and deserted hole in the ground, and it is even less comforting when we face death ourselves. Many of us secretly wish the fundamentalists could be right.

The problem, however, is that neither point of view concerning heaven is very satisfying. The fundamentalists limit heaven to the next world; the liberals limit heaven to this world. Neither really helps.

The words of Jesus to his disciples and to us do not settle the confusion and controversy of what heaven is like. Our Lord refuses to give either the temperature of hell or describe the furniture of heaven. Why should he? For after all, it doesn't do any good to know exactly what heaven is like unless we have the certainty of going there. This is where we need to start.

Room Enough

Not many hours ago Jesus had washed the disciples' feet as a sign of their servanthood here on earth. Now he is in the process of cleansing their minds of old ideas. He knows that the mere mention of heaven as a goal will create all kinds of misconceptions in the minds of his disciples. Being good Jews, the disciples thought of heaven as restricted real estate. The big issue for them was not the question of the existence of heaven, but — is there room enough for them in heaven? Their fear of a shortage of housing in heaven closed their minds to the idea that anyone other than a good Jew could get in.

Like the disciples, our ideas about heaven are often

too narrow or in some cases, too broad. Either we think of heaven as being ultra *exclusive*, like a Hall of Fame where only a few outstanding pious people are admitted, or else our view of heaven is all *inclusive* — a no-reservation-needed resort, like a public park where everyone is admitted free.

Jesus ignores both of these extreme exaggerations of the hereafter and presents his own unique view. He proclaims heaven to be both exclusive and inclusive. Heaven is *exclusive* in that there is only one door into heaven and he is it. At the same time heaven is *inclusive*, because it is splendidly spacious with room enough for all.

When our Lord says, "I go to prepare a place for you," the focus of our Lord's attention is not on the word "place" but on the words "I" and "you." He adds, "I will come again and take you unto myself that where I am you may be also." Heaven is neither a *place* nor a condition of the moral structure of existence. Rather, heaven is *space in the heart of God.* It is our own exclusive room in the inclusive heart of God. Our space, our room in the house of God, is made for us, and it will fit no one else.

To further define this space in the heart of God, Christ points to himself. He says, "I am the way, the truth and the life." Here again the scholars ponder the meaning of these words and wonder, while believers cling to these words and hope.

The Way

First, the *way.* The traditional interpretation of this word is that Jesus is saying that he is the guide and the path. Therefore we are to follow Christ, and he will lead us to heaven. Like the children's game of *Follow the Leader,* we do what he does, and we go where he goes. Follow the blood-stained footprints of the shepherd-savior and he will lead us like sheep safely back into the fold.

There is much truth in this directive to follow Christ and imitate his life, if we would please God and do his will. But the testimony of many well-intentioned strivers after this perfection is that we *cannot*. Try as hard as we can — we cannot. Even Paul admits that what he would do, he does not. We have the will, but no will *power*, because we are a broken people in a fallen and fractured world.

This hard saying of Christ, however, can have another meaning. A way, a path, a road carries traffic in both directions. When Christ says, "I am the way," he could mean that he is the way to go to God, or he could mean he is the way God comes to us — or both. A careful study of the lessons for the day would suggest that Christ really means the latter. Our Lord is saying that he is the way we come to God, and at the same time, he is the way God comes to us. Heaven moves in upon us in the person of Jesus Christ. God the Father comes to us in Jesus Christ and takes us into himself. That is truly heaven — being encountered, chosen and taken by God into himself.

When we think of a ladder or a set of stairs, our first thought is that they are means of climbing up. But a ladder or stairs is used for both movements — up and down. We sing, "I am climbing Jacob's ladder," and overlook the fact that in the Scriptures, Jacob's ladder enabled the angels to both descend and ascend.

The interpretation that presents Jesus as the way God comes to us is much more meaningful and helpful. We are soiled and sin-stained. We are like people fallen into a pit. In the fall we are injured. Our legs and arms are broken. To lower a ladder to us and say — "This is the way out. Climb it." — only adds to our desperation. But if the ladder is lowered into the pit, not for us to climb out, but that one might climb down to us and lift our broken body into his arms, carrying us upward and out to safety and salvation — this is good news.

Such a view of Christ as the way is consistent not only with the whole concept of our helpless state of sin, but with God's incarnate act in Christ who comes to us where we are and lifts and carries us unto himself. "I will come and take you," says the Lord.

Christ is the *way*. Not just our way to God, which is in the experience of untold pilgrims an impossible route for helpless sinners, but God's way *to* us, which is the good news of God's coming to us as redeemer and Lord.

The Truth

Next, our Lord says that he is the *truth*. When we hear the word "truth," we think in terms of a reliable set of truths. We think of facts and assertions that can be logically formulated, rationally understood, tested and proven. This static form of truth gives stability to our existence. Without it, life would be chaos.

When Christ uses the word "truth," however, it is not a static proposition but a dynamic action. Christ is the truth not because of what he says alone, but because of what he does. "I do the will of him who sent me," says the Lord. Christ does the truth — the truth of the Father. All that Christ did was directed by the will of God the Father. Complete conformity and absolute obedience to the Father is the truth that the Lord identifies with.

The opposite of static truth is falsehood. The opposite of the truth which is Christ is faithlessness. We should add, the full meaning of Christ as truth includes not only what he says and does, but who he is.

In our present-day culture, the opposite of truth is "phoney" — people who pretend with words and deeds to be what they are not. Christ is not a phoney. He is authentic. Christ *is* what he says and does. What our Lord says and does is a mirrored reflection of who he is.

The tragic aspect of truth in the form of facts is that

we can so easily conclude that hearing the truth, we have it — possess it with a certainty and a security that needs nothing else except the possession of that truth. It follows from such a position that the only thing left for us to do is to apply the truth, develop programs and plans to put this truth into action.

Truth, as Christ is the truth, is never under the control of our little minds. Nor can it ever be possessed in our tightly grasped fists. Truth is a living person, one who daily confronts us and with whom we must struggle and wrestle as Jacob did with the angel until we are blessed. Christ is a truth we do not possess, but a truth which relentlessly pursues us until it possesses *us*. This means that each day we encounter this truth anew.

As the "way" means that Christ is God's way of coming to us, "truth" means God's determination to change us when he does come to us.

When Christ proclaims that he is the truth, all of our programs and plans and priorities are called into question. We are shaken, as Tillich says, to our very "foundations." But we rejoice in such an attacking, aggressive, dynamic form of truth, for such truth and such truth alone gives life.

A deep-sea fisherman always returned to the docks at the end of the day with all of his catch of fish fresh and alive. Many people wondered what the secret was of keeping caught fish alive. When the old fisherman was about to die, he passed on his secret. He said, "I always take along some fighting catfish in the tank of my boat, and they attack the caught fish and keep them active and alive."

So our encounter with Christ as living truth — active and dynamic truth — creates the confrontation and conflict that keeps us and our faith alive. Which brings us to the third term our Lord applies to himself.

The Life

Christ says, "I am the life." For many of us the belief that Christ is the *way* and the *truth* reflects a narrow concern for our own souls and our own personal salvation. When the Bible speaks of salvation, we think of "saved souls." We limit the concern of God to some divine spark within us — some Casper-like ghost that is imprisoned in our sinful bodies and whom God rescues and sets free to fly back to heaven. Heaven becomes a personal goal — a place where "I am going when I die."

Some people sing with gusto, "Jesus Saviour, pilot me," and we cannot help but wonder if this does not mean, "Save me Lord — just me, O Lord, and let others go their merry way to hell." Such an attitude is not only far from our Lord's meaning when he says, "I am the way, the truth and the life," but it is unworthy of all who would name Christ as their savior and Lord.

All of Life

When Christ says that he is the *life*, he means that he is bringing to us a new and bigger life. He is not talking about "saved souls" but about saved persons. Christ brings a salvation that involves all of life — the whole of life. It is a new life of the soul and the body. It is a life for the individual and for the world. It is both personal and social, immediate and ultimate, universal and particular. It is historical, eschatological and eternal. It is a past promise, a daily experience, and a final hope. Nothing in all the world and no one living or dead or yet unborn is beyond the scope of Christ as the giver of life.

Jesus in this passage is not speculating about life here, now, or hereafter; he is bringing life, giving life, a bigger and a better life — now!

When Jesus was born, angels hailed him a savior for all people everywhere. Holding him in his arms, the aged

Simeon cried out, "My eyes have seen salvation." Not just salvation for Israel but for all people — everywhere. Preaching in the wilderness, John the Baptizer reached the climax of his message when he proclaimed, "All flesh shall see the salvation of God."

When Jesus began to preach, he spoke in terms of his coming as an event of gigantic proportions: good news to the poor; release to the captives; sight to the blind; setting at liberty those who are oppressed; proclaiming the year of the Lord; the Kingdom of God has come! With bold strokes, he covered the broad canvas of existence with a brilliant rainbow of colors encompassing the whole spectrum of light — the light which is life itself.

Wholeness of Life

Christ means wholeness of life. Wherever Christ went, life took on a deeper and fuller meaning. True life, abundant life, was released by his words, his touch, his acts of love. Christ was life before the world began, and for us Christ is life now, authentic life, free from fear and frustration, free from anxiety and despair, free from legalism and petty rules, free from wrong attitudes and false gods, free from sin, and guilt, and shame, and ultimately free from the greatest enemy of all — death itself. "For me to live is Christ," shouts Paul, and the whole host of heaven shouts back, "Amen!"

So Christ says, "I am the way, the truth and the life." As the *way* means God's way to us — as *truth* means God's determination to change us — so *life* means God's gift of a new and better life to us. Christ is making the fantastic claim that he is God. By his life and death and resurrection, he opens wide the very heart of the eternal God and reveals there a reserved space for us, space in the heart of God where we might live forever.

On a stormy night, an elderly man and his wife entered the lobby of a small hotel in Philadelphia. The clerk explained there were three conventions in town and there were no rooms to be had anywhere in the city.

Then the clerk noticed the despair and even fear as the old couple glanced at each other. The clerk was moved. He smiled and said, "I can't turn you out in the storm at this late hour, so if you don't mind the inconvenience of a small room, you can have mine and I will sleep here in the lobby."

The couple replied that they appreciated his offer, but they could not ask him to make such a sacrifice. The clerk replied, "It is no sacrifice. I want to do it."

The next morning as the elderly man paid his bill, he said to the clerk, "You are the kind of a person who should manage the biggest and best hotel in the United States. Maybe — just maybe — someday I'll build one for you."

Two years passed and the young man had forgotten the incident when a letter came to him from a law firm in New York City. The letter was short and to the point, informing him that he was to manage a new hotel which was to be America's finest. The letter added that the hotel had actually been built by the owner for him to manage. It would be called the Waldorf-Astoria.

The young man let out a yell of jubilation and then became suddenly silent as he remembered that stormy night two years ago when he had given up his room to an elderly couple, and he recalled the casual words the man had spoken, "Maybe someday I'll build you a hotel." The clerk raced through the back records and sure enough there were the names — Mr. and Mrs. William Waldorf Astor.

Two thousand years ago during a storm at mid-day on a hill called Calvary, a young man hung on a cross. He willingly gave up his life in obedience to God the Father. He did it not for himself, but for *us*! Because of that deed, God built into the very structure of heaven a room especially prepared for us.

There is much about heaven we cannot understand. There is too much for our minds to comprehend in our Lord's statement that he is the *way,* the *truth* and the *life.* But of one thing we can be certain — when we face death, we do not face the bad news of a grim reaper with sickle in hand ready to cut us down and destroy us. Rather we face the good news of a savior and in his hand is a cross, and that cross is the key that unlocks for us our personal room in the house of God our Father. Christ by his sacrifice creates and gives to us *space* in the heart of God. Here we shall dwell in love and joy forever. This really is good news!

God in Us

SIXTH SUNDAY OF EASTER
John 14:15-21

Many of us have a teeter-totter theology. God sits on one end and we sit on the other. When God acts, he pushes down on his end. We react by pushing down on our end.

The way we play this game of theological teeter-totter varies. Those who are moralists teach that we must push down on our end first. We act and God reacts. We believe in God and he responds by saving us. We confess our sins and God forgives us. We are good and obedient, and God reacts by blessing us with the things we ask for.

The more evangelical approach reverses the process. God first acts by saving us, and we respond by believing in him. God forgives first, and as a result of this forgiveness, we confess that we have sinned. God blesses us, and we in turn strive to be obedient and do his will.

With the first words of our Gospel today, Jesus comes down heavy on our end of the teeter-totter. Jesus says, "Love me and keep my commandments."

We do not know what the reaction of the disciples was to this new demand of our Lord. We do know that his claims upon the disciples increased with intensity as their relationship developed with the Lord.

When the disciples first encountered Jesus, he simply asked them to follow him. He didn't ask them to believe in him or trust him or even to love him. He just said to them, "Follow me," and they did.

As their relationship developed, our Lord asked the disciples to open their ears and listen to him. They responded as best they could. We know that they followed him along the dusty roads and through the crowded villages. As they walked and he talked, they listened to him. They didn't always understand. In fact, from our historic perspective and accumulated knowledge of the Scriptures, we could easily conclude that they understood very little of the real thrust of his message and mission. When he made reference to his suffering and death followed by a miracle of resurrection, the point of it all was completely lost to the disciples.

The disciples, like most of us, were people of the earth — practical people. Any talk of salvation, a new kingdom, glory and power, was in the minds of the disciples one dimensional — limited to this world only. Freedom meant liberation from Roman rule. A kingdom meant Christ on a throne in Jerusalem with the disciples standing beside him as ruling princes of a new realm. It all sounded good to the disciples, and they were eager to discover what they had to do to be a part of it all.

Everywhere they went, the disciples encountered people who shared their teeter-totter theology. The crowds flocked to Jesus always asking the same question, "What must I do to inherit the kingdom?" They were alike in the desire to know how to push down on their end of the teeter-totter so that God would react and release for them a kingdom.

The answers Jesus gave became more and more demanding until, as we find in our text today, the demands for a place in the kingdom became unmanageable.

Love Me — Keep My Commandments

Last Sunday in our Gospel lesson we heard Jesus

telling the disciples that they must believe in him and trust him. In our Gospel today, Jesus says that they must love him and keep his commandments.

It is surprising to note that the theme or the demand that the disciples love Jesus is not common until the last days of their relationship. Most of the time, Jesus talked about their need to love God the Father. But now that he is coming to the end of his ministry here on earth, he tells the disciples, "Love me."

Even though this is a decisive change, the demand did not sound too severe to the disciples — nor to us. If all we have to do to push down our end of the teeter-totter is to love Jesus, we have it made. After all, Jesus is the most lovable character in all of history. Even those who are unwilling to acknowledge him as the divine Son of God quite readily admit that he is a completely admirable and lovable person. Few can resist the Bethlehem babe in a crib or the young man of Calvary valiantly giving his life on a cross for others.

However, Jesus doesn't stop with the demand that he be loved; he adds a description of this love. Jesus says, "If you love me, you will keep my commandments." Our Lord describes the kind of love he has in mind, a love expressed by keeping his commandments. This means that loving Jesus and being obedient to his will are the same thing. Loving Jesus is easy, particularly when we are convinced by our teeter-totter theology that such loving will work the lever that gets us all we want — health and happiness here on earth, and a secure spot in heaven when we die. But keeping his commandments, that is a different ball game. The price of the kingdom goes up, up to inflation heights, particularly when we realize the radical dimensions of his demands.

The Ten Commandments are difficult to fulfill to the letter, but not altogether impossible to obey in principle. But when Jesus adds his interpretation to the commandments, they are impossible, staggering in their demands.

For example: "Thou shalt not kill" is a difficult commandment in a hostile world where we need to preserve our way of life from aggressive and ambitious nations who threaten to take away our freedoms.

Within our own personal lives it is somewhat easier. We have to be pushed to extreme anger before we consider killing someone who has done ill against us. But Jesus isn't satisfied with a non-violent life. He says that if we hate or become angry with another person we are, in the sight of God, guilty of having killed him.

The commandments, according to Jesus, push moral performance to the point of perfection. Before such a devastating demand our neat little teeter-totter theology breaks down. Who can honestly say that she has never disliked a disagreeable person and wished her out of the way? Or who has not entertained revenge as a welcomed guest in his heart?

Will Rogers is quoted as saying, "I never met a man I didn't like." His son, however, pointed out in a public interview that this was a misquote. What his father actually said was, "I never met *with* a man I didn't like." That little word "with" makes quite a difference. It means that Will Rogers was not any different than most of us who find the best answer to eliminating anger in our lives is to avoid situations and people who arouse it in us.

We all *try* to do what is right. We all want to do what is right. But for our Lord, the road to heaven is not paved with good intentions — the road to hell is. The acid test of our love for Jesus is not good intentions but perfect performance. He offers us no escape from the law but interprets the law so that we cannot possibly escape being judged by it.

Trying Our Best — Not Good Enough

When Peter O'Toole, the actor, was asked how he

would like to be remembered, he answered by relating a story about his favorite jacket. It was a cherished possession, worn and stained by years of wearing. Ashamed to wear it in public, he reluctantly sent it to the cleaners. When the coat was returned, it was obvious from the identifying ticket that it had been sent to several branches of the cleaning establishment. There was a short note attached to the jacket: "We regret to return an article less than perfect, but we tried our best."

"We tried our best." Is this not a parable about where we hope we might stand before God on that final day of judgment — among those who tried their best? But Jesus does not say to the disciples, "If you love me, you will try your best to keep my commandments." No. He pulls no punches. His statement is direct and to the point. "If you love me, you will *keep* my commandments."

The perfection Jesus demands is for us an impossibility. We are too soiled and stained by sin. So where does that leave us? High in the air on our end of the teeter-totter with no weight or force or power to push our end down. In fact it pushes us right off of the teeter-totter of righteousness and leaves us helpless — unable to even get off the ground.

A Helper

Jesus, however, doesn't stop with this statement of loving him by keeping his commandments. He goes on to say that God will send us a *helper*. Originally, the Greek word used here was "parakletos" or paraclete. In the Latin translations it became "advocatus," which means one "called in" to help or advise — an advocate. Sometimes in the English translations, the word "counselor" is used. At other times the choice is "intercessor." In our text, Jesus refers to the "Spirit of truth," one who will bear witness of Christ in the hearts of the believers. In the context of St. John's Gospel, it really refers to the Holy Spirit.

However you translate this word, it refers to God giving himself to us in our time of need. God does for us what we cannot do for ourselves. The important point that must not be overlooked is that this is not just an announcement of the coming of help from God, but the fact that God himself will come and enter *into* us and dwell *within* us.

The whole thrust of our Gospel this morning is the *indwelling* of God *in* us. Verse twenty of our text is the key: "I am *in* my Father and you *in* me and I *in* you." God *in* us! This is the gospel. This is the good news! When the full force of this good news hits us, it turns our teeter-totter theology topsy-turvy. It literally turns an impossible demand into a *premium promise*. For there is a vast difference between *doing* God's will, and God's will *done* in us! In the first case we do something. In the latter, something is done to us.

God on Both Ends

The total message of what our Lord says adds up to the astounding realization that our salvation does not depend on us or our efforts, but is a gift of grace given by God. From now on we view God on both ends of the teeter-totter of redemption. Instead of God acting and then we reacting, the *wholeness* of God in the process of redemption is proclaimed. A new teeter-totter principle is introduced, not with us on one end and God on the other, but with God on one end acting *for* us, and on the other end — our end — God acting *in* us. God gives what God demands.

In the life, death and resurrection of our Lord, God acts *for* our salvation. Then, by means of the gift of the Holy Spirit, God acts *in* us. God comes to our end of the teeter-totter in the word proclaimed and in the sacraments of communion and baptism, giving us the power to have belief and faith and love, and in this experience, to be obedient to our Lord's commands and thereby love him.

Response-ability

You may ask, does this mean we have no personal responsibility in this process of redemption? Is Christ saying that we need not respond to what God has done for us? No. Rather it shows to us that responsibility in the New Testament sense is made up of two words — "response" and "ability." It faces honestly the fact that because we are broken sinners living in a fallen world, we have no personal ability in and of ourselves to make the necessary and demanded response to God; therefore, God sends to us a "helper" — the Holy Spirit — and the resulting *indwelling* of God in us gives us the *ability* to respond. This is the good news of a new *responsibility*, a responsibility not based on human righteousness but a righteousness resulting from a new relationship between God and ourselves. The holiness of God is revealed in his *wholeness*. He is totally involved in our redemption. He does not stand outside us working for us. He enters into us and works a miracle of faith within us. We become new persons, God-filled people, who exercise a new responsibility by surrendering to the God who enters into us and lays total claim upon us. This is the good news. This is the new responsibility. This is the new gospel of Christ our Lord.

If God is on both ends of the teeter-totter, this may be a new view of the gospel, but is it really good news for us as persons? Are we not destroyed as responsible persons in the whole process? Again the answer is "no." We do not become pious puppets performing appropriately when our divine strings are pulled. The indwelling of God in us does not destroy our personal identity or integrity. Just the opposite. In our union with God we become fulfilled as persons — we become in the truest sense the persons we were intended to be.

In the marriage relationship, we proclaim the extraordinary mathematics that one plus one equals one. However, the experience of becoming "one" does not destroy our maleness or our femaleness but actually fulfills them. So God entering into us does not destroy our uniqueness as a person but actually makes it possible. We become the whole person we were intended to be from the time of our creation.

We are created by our very nature not to dwell in isolation on one end of a celestial teeter-totter; we are not like Hercamedies who faces the impossible task of operating a lever that will move the immovable God. We are not created to be alone either in this earthly existence or in the spiritual relationship we have with God. Without others around us, we are alone and unfulfilled in this life. Without God in us, not only is our life empty and meaningless, but we are empty within ourselves, hollow people, only a shell of what we should be.

God in Us

It is important to note that what our Lord is saying is not just that God comes to us and exists near us or beside us or even with us, but the extraordinary revelation that God comes to dwell *in us*. Jesus is not talking about God in our world but God in us. This is the gospel. For it is not what is outside of us that influences us and gives us power, but what is in us.

We all know that we can be alone in a crowd. We can be lonely even though there are people all about us. Mrs. Cornelius Vanderbilt, Sr., lived in a fifty-eight room Fifth Avenue mansion. In all that splendor she once wrote to a friend: "Yesterday I was so lonely. I spent the entire day alone in the house." The truth is there were eighteen servants in the house when Mrs. Vanderbilt wrote that she was alone.

It isn't our environment, no matter how splendid or populated, that solves our basic problem of loneliness, because loneliness is an *inward* state. Even in a crowded church with evidences of God all about us in stone and song, liturgy and scripture, prayer and fellowship, we can be *alone,* apart from God unless he is willing to enter *into* us and *fill* us with his living presence.

This presence of God within us is what Jesus is talking about in our Gospel text today. The disciples had been with Jesus for three years. They had lived beside him, walked with him, even touched and embraced him, but that was not enough. They needed more than companionship with the Lord to face the destiny that lay ahead of them. They needed an intimate *communion in* their Lord. This our Lord accomplished on the cross and by his resurrection and ascension, but most of all, by his sending to the disciples a spirit to dwell within them.

Here within these last conversations with the disciples, Christ is assuring them that they are in for a new and greater relationship with him than they had ever known. Up to this time, they had only been with him. Now his leaving and coming again in the Holy Spirit meant that the disciples were about to experience the life-fulfilling thrill of being *in* him and he in them. That same promise God is making to us today.

How like children we are, being content to have God with us. How easy it is to be content with a teeter-totter theology where religion is so simple. God acts and we react. It is so neat and nice, but in our satisfied immaturity, we miss the thrill of the wholeness of life that Christ so willingly desires to give to us.

The whole New Testament testifies to the fact that Christ brings a new way, a new commandment, a new life. The essence of that life is the action of God acting not only *for* us but *in* us. Christ came that we might know God. Christ comes again in the Holy Spirit that we might experience God within us. This is the good news of Christ's going away — a new relationship with God for the disciples and us, a new relationship, not just being with God but in God and he in us.

A father came home from work utterly exhausted. He went directly to the bedroom and stretched out across the bed.

His two sons, a six-year old and a seven-year old, came in from play. The first thing they asked was, "Is Daddy home?"

Their mother assured them that he was, but that he was very tired and was resting in his room, and they should not disturb him.

When their mother left the room, the two little boys headed for the hall and walked slowly by the open door of their parent's bedroom. Sure enough, there was their father apparently asleep.

Not satisfied, the two boys made another trip past the bedroom, and this time they stopped and tiptoed into the room. They went over and stood silently by the bed.

"Don't get too close" the older boy warned. But his younger brother paid no notice. He went over to the side of the bed and put his face right over the face of his father. He turned his head and tried to look under his father's eyelids. Finally, he reached up, and with one finger slowly lifted the lid of his father's eye and peered in as if he were looking into a deep hole.

Then turning to his older brother, he said, "he's still in there."

Is this not a parable of our relationship with God? Despite all the witness of the Scriptures and the church that God is present in our world, we still want more assurance. We would like to lift the closed eyelids that cover the mystery of God's presence and peer in to see if God is still with us.

We will never be given such a vision, but the good news of the gospel is the promise that God is not only in our world but he is in us. He dwells within us so that we might know him, truly know him, not only as one who loved us so much that he died for us, but one who loved us so much he came to live in us.

The certainty of our salvation is not the evidence of history that he is in the world, or the testimony of saints that he is in the church, or the evidence of scholars that he is in the Bible, but the assurance and promise of our Lord and Savior, Jesus Christ, that God is *in us* and we are *in him.*

"I am in my Father
and you in me,
and I in you."

Man-made teeter-totter theologies crash down around our heads, and in our hearts is raised a cross and a crown, and God becomes alive in us.

The Seated Saviour

THE ASCENSION OF OUR LORD
Luke 24:44-53

Did you ever stop to think about the symbolism of a
chair — an ordinary, everyday chair? It really plays a
very important role in our lives.

When we are young and start school, we are assigned
a chair on a seating chart. We are marked present or
absent according to whether or not we occupy *our* chair.

As adults we attend important social activities — a
concert, a ball-game, the theater, a formal dinner, in
comfort and style if we have a reserved seat.

Like Archie Bunker, we all have our favorite chairs
for watching TV or just relaxing at home. In church
many of us sit in the same place, in the same pew,
Sunday after Sunday, and are even offended when
someone else occupies our accustomed place.

We feel comfortable sitting in a familiar spot, a place
we can call our own. That is what gives the particular
personal meaning to a chair. It is *our* chair, our *place*.
More than any other article of furniture, a chair
represents and defines *our space* in the impersonal
environment of our existence.

In the history of our culture, the chair has been
symbolic, not only of personal space, but as a mark of
power and authority.

In the field of education, the chair stands for the

teaching office. In academic circles we talk about a person occupying the chair of philosophy or history or literature.

In the history of the church, the chair has been the symbol of the pastoral office of the bishop. Long before the altar was the focal point of worship, the bishop's chair — called a cathedra — was placed in front of the worshiping assembly and represented the authority of the presence of Christ. The bishop preached his sermon seated in the cathedra, thereby giving his words the authority of one chosen by God to speak. We still refer to an authentic utterance as "speaking ex-cathedra" and refer to important churches as "cathedrals" — the "place of the chair."

In the governmental structure of most civilizations from the earliest of times, a chair — called a throne — was the symbol of the power and prestige of royal rule. He who occupies the throne is divinely destined to direct the affairs of state.

Now why all this talk about chairs and sitting in a sermon about Ascension Day? Well, the interesting and often overlooked fact is that the theological meaning of the Ascension centers on three chairs claimed by Christ when he ascends in his state of glory — the chair of prophet, the chair of priest, and the chair of king.

The Seated Saviour

In the creed, when we refer to the act of Christ's Ascension, we confess, "He ascended into heaven, and sitteth on the right hand of God the Father Almighty." Now, of course, God does not have a right hand, nor is there a chair beside his throne where our Lord sits, but this is the picture language used by believers to confess that Jesus, who put aside his might and majesty at Christmas, now once more assumes his eternal position of power as the Son of God and the Savior of all creation.

Picture language is not unusual. We say that the sun "rises and sets," knowing full well that the sun doesn't literally rise in the east and set in the west. It is we who move, not the sun. But such picture language communicates accurately what we experience. So when the early divines of our faith desired to picture for us their experience of the victory of the risen Lord, they pictured him as ascending into the clouds and above the clouds into heaven where he sits to reign at the right hand of God.

The event of the Ascension was foretold in the ascension-picture of Elijah, sailing off into the clouds in a fiery chariot (2 Kings 2:9-15) and in the picture-language of the Psalms of praise (Psalm 47 and 68). The first three Gospels, Matthew (28:16-20), Mark (16:19-20), and Luke (24:50-53), conclude with accounts of the Ascension. The fourth Gospel, though it does not describe the event, does include Christ's announcement to Mary at the empty tomb that, "I am ascending to my Father and your Father, to my God, and your God." (John 20:17) The book of Revelation (1:1, 2:5-6) is a vision given by the Ascended Lord. Peter was impressed with the importance of the Ascension (1 Peter 3:22), and Paul testified to its profound doctrinal value (Ephesians 4:10). In the basic structure of the New Testament, the Ascension is the connecting link between the life of Christ and the life of the church. From its anticipation in Genesis (5:24) to its recollection in Revelation, the Ascension is regarded as a decisive act in the work of redemption. It all comes to focus in the creedal confession, "He ascended into heaven, and *sitteth* on the right hand of God the Father Almighty." Christ is the *Seated Savior.* He sits on three chairs of power and authority — the chair of prophecy — the chair of priesthood — the chair of kingly glory.

Let us look at these three chairs which symbolize the meaning of the Ascension for us, because each represents a vital aspect and action of the personhood of our Lord.

As Prophet, he is sent from God. As Priest, he returns to God. As King, he is ruler with God.

Three Chairs for Christ

The first is the chair of prophecy. Christ was a prophet sent from God. We commonly think of a prophet as one who sees into the future and foretells events which are to come, but in the truest sense of the word, a prophet is one who penetrates into the deep meanings of the present — one who is given a special, divinely inspired insight into the status of our existence in relationship to God our Father. We all know that we have problems in this area of faith and belief. We don't need anyone to proclaim to us the obvious, or to teach us what we already know from experience; but a prophet is one sent from God with a unique revelation, and who possesses the creative genius of penetrating to the heart of our problems and presenting to us the divinely given solution.

A true prophet comes to us as a teacher revealing to us not only our predicament, but at the same time, offering to us the grace of a saving solution.

The president of the Pontiac Division of General Motors received the following letter from a customer:

Every night after my family has eaten dinner, we vote on what kind of ice cream we should have for dessert and I immediately drive down to the store and get it.

Recently I purchased a new Pontiac and since then my trips to the store have created a problem. Everytime I buy vanilla ice cream, when I start back home from the store, my car won't start. If I get any other flavor of ice cream, the car starts fine.

I want you to know I'm serious about this

question, no matter how silly it sounds:
What is it about a Pontiac that makes it not
start when I get vanilla and easy to start
when I get any other flavor of ice cream?"

The president of Pontiac was understandably
skeptical about the letter, but at the same time was
intrigued by it. So he sent an engineer to check it out.

The engineer went with the man to the store four
nights. The first night the man got vanilla. The car failed
to start. The second night the man got chocolate. The car
started. The third night he got strawberry. The car
started. The fourth night, vanilla, and the car failed to
start.

The engineer, being a logical man, refused to believe
that a Pontiac car could be allergic to vanilla ice cream.
He arranged, therefore, to continue his investigation as
long as it might take to solve the problem. He took
careful notes: the time of day, type of gas used, time
needed to drive back and forth, etc.

Eventually, the engineer discovered the clue to the
solution of the problem; the man took more *time* to buy
any other flavor than vanilla. Why? The answer was in
the layout of the store. Being the most popular flavor,
vanilla ice cream was in a separate case in the front of
the store for easy pickup.

Once time was identified with the problem — not
vanilla ice cream — the engineer quickly came up with
the answer — vapor lock. The extra time taken to get the
other flavors allowed the engine to cool down sufficiently
to start. When the man got vanilla, the engine was still
too hot for the vapor lock to dissipate.

Long before Jesus came onto the scene, we knew that
something was wrong at the center of life. Every time we
attempted righteousness, we stalled, and our life just
wouldn't start. But we didn't know why. We had the

Ten Commandments. We knew right from wrong. But the more we would try to please God and do his will, the more we realized how far short from his demanded perfection we were falling.

Then Jesus came, teaching us that our understanding of sin and wrongdoing was shallow and superficial. We were concerned only with outward actions and attempted to train ourselves and bring our lives into line with God's will. Jesus made it clear that the root of our problem was not outward actions of breaking the laws and rules and regulations, but our real problem was the vapor-lock within us. Not what we did, but who we are.

Our problem is that ultimately everything we do centers in self. Even the good we do is done to make us good. Outwardly we are law-abiding, Bible-reading, commandment-following, go-to-church-on-Sunday Christians; but inwardly, we do it all not to please God or serve others but to get what we want.

Our problem is inner secret desires: the sin of trying to be better than other people; the sin of trying to get a bigger house, a more expensive car, a higher salary than the person beside us; the sin of pushing our way ahead regardless of whom we have to step on; the sin of getting our own way by force, by cruelty, if need be, even by violence, if necessary; the sin of putting our trust in transient things like a slick stock market deal, a bulging bank account, and a sure-pay insurance program; the sin of judging others and ignoring the faults in ourselves; the sin of satisfying our own desires at the expense of others; the sin of using people rather than serving them.

This penetrating insight of our Lord into the real problem area of our life — our inward self — identified him as the true prophet and teacher sent from God. He brought to light the real cause of our alienation from God; not the sins that we do but the sinners we are. We attempt to play God in our own lives and in the lives of others.

Our Lord spoke as one with authority because he got under our skin and into our hearts and minds and revealed the problem to be a vapor-lock of personal pride and self-centeredness.

The Ascension was the culmination of all our Lord's teachings dramatically acted out before us — that the key to life is not self-service but God's acceptance. We need to have an ascension within our own lives. We need to be lifted up and out of our selfishness. We need to be taken up — lifted out of our entanglement with things that rust and rot and are eaten by moths. We need to rise above this earthly life, and this can happen only when our vapor-locked pride is broken and our trust in things is denied and we turn to God as the only source of all true life. This is what the Ascension of Christ means to us. He is the prophet of life, the master teacher of life, and his words bring life. In him we too can be lifted up to a new life, an abundant and joyful life of obedience to the God who made us. We can, because of his Ascension, ascend out of our sinful, vapor-locked state and start again to become the people God intended us to be.

Chair of Priest

The second chair of our Lord's Ascension is the chair of Priest. As prophet and teacher, he not only penetrates to the heart of our problem and lays bear the true nature of our sin, but he does something about it. He heals it. He cleanses our unrighteousness. As a high priest greater than Aaron or Melchizedeck, he makes the supreme sacrifice, the once-for-all offering to God, and thereby heals and makes us whole. He goes obediently to the altar of the cross and becomes the spotless lamb slain for our transgressions. He willingly lays down his life on Golgotha that we might rise up and live. His body broken and his blood spilled become the one, perfect, unrepeatable sacrifice to end the need for all other sacrifices. Triumphantly he encounters death and compassionately gives unending life.

The Ascension, however, means so much more to us. Our Lord is pictured in the Ascension as our advocate, sitting at the right hand of God, not standing in the posture of a suppliant leaving us in doubt as to the outcome of our judgment, but sitting as the High Priest exercising absolute authority. Here by the power of this chair of priesthood he constantly intercedes for us before the judgment throne of God the Father.

The key word here for our understanding of the Ascension is the word *constantly.* It is not enough that we be forgiven once. We are so fragile in our faith. Try as we will, we continually fumble and fail and fall. We need continual forgiveness — not just a liturgical production at the font; but a day-by-day process that only begins with the outward act of baptism and is continued as a day-by-day experience of being constantly forgiven.

Luther points out that at our baptism the old man in us is drowned, but he is a good swimmer and needs to be daily dunked — daily brought under the cleansing waters of holy baptism.

A wealthy English family invited some friends to spend the holiday on their beautiful estate. An almost tragic thing happened the first day. While the children were swimming, one of them began to drown. The others screamed for help. Fortunately, one of the gardeners heard the screams, jumped into the pool and saved the drowning boy — Winston Churchill.

Winston's parents asked the gardener what they could do to reward him. He answered that he wanted nothing for himself, but he had a son who wanted to go to college and study to be a doctor. "We will gladly pay his way through," answered Churchill's grateful parents.

Some years later, when Churchill was Prime Minister of England, he was stricken with pneumonia. The king, much alarmed, sent for the best physician in the land.

The doctor summoned was Sir Alexander Fleming, the developer of penicillin. His medical skill and his new drug saved Winston Churchill's life. To Winston's surprise, Dr. Fleming was the son of the gardener who had saved Winston as a child.

"Rarely," said Churchill later, "has one man owed his life twice to the same person."

Churchill was right when he said that rarely do we owe our physical life twice to the same person; but in the realm of faith, we owe our life a thousand times over to one man — Jesus Christ. He not only dies once for us on Calvary and offers his body and blood for our atonement, but he eternally sits at the right hand of God and makes constant intercession for us.

Each time that we kneel at the Lord's table and partake of his sacramental supper, we experience again and again the continual forgiveness he so willingly and freely gives to us.

The Ascension is a festival of this continuing forgiveness. Christ, sitting at the right hand of God as priest, is our certain hope and assurance that we can daily ascend above the guilt of our sins and rise from our knees again and again to begin a fresh new life each day.

The Chair of King

The third chair of our Lord's Ascension is that of king. As prophet and teacher, Christ reveals the vapor-lock corruption of our sinfulness. As priest he daily makes intercession for our transgressions and heals the wounds we daily inflict upon ourselves. Now as king, he rules with God and gives us the ability to rise above the chaotic world of antagonistic forces that threaten to overpower us.

We so easily think of Christ in the one dimension of his common humanity — peasant son of a carpenter, friend of smelly fishermen, a rural rabbi who walks the dusty back-roads of Palestine in his rugged homespun robe, quietly teaching the truth of God, challenging the pedantic pride of the Pharisees, condemning the elaborate ritual of the priests and the liturgical extravagancies of the temple.

We picture our Lord as the "gentle Jesus" — the humble "Servant Savior," with bowl and towel, washing the dirty feet of his disciples and silently submitting to the ignominious death of a criminal on a cruel cross. This is a true picture of our Lord, but it is only a one-dimensional view. It is only a partial picture of our Lord, particularly when we fail to project our vision into the future where the regal Christ reigns as king.

Christ is not only the suffering servant of Isaiah; he is also the exulted victor of Revelation.

The problem most of us have with our Lord's kingship is the factual condition of the broken world in which we have to live. How in the face of all the atrocities and the suffering of innocents can Christ rule as commander and chief? A world populated with babies bloated by starvation, bloody battlefields strewn with broken bodies, intrigue and corruption in high places, crime and senseless brutality stalking the dark shadows of our streets, cancer-ridden patients knowing only terminal pain — how in the midst of all this can we confess in a Risen and Ascended Lord, sitting in power and majesty above it all?

The truth is — we cannot. We cannot believe in a triumphant Lord of love unless our vision ascends above the time and place of this present world to the world that is to come.

Before Columbus discovered the New World, the coat of arms of Spain bore the motto: *Ne Plus Ultra,* which means, "There is nothing beyond." The three-mile limit of their shore line was the limit of their utmost horizon and furthest possibilities. But after Columbus had braved the terrors of the unknown and uncharted sea and discovered America, the *Ne* was dropped from the Spanish coat of arms, leaving only the motto: *Plus Ultra* — "There is more beyond."

So our Lord pioneered through the veil of tears and beyond the horizons of this world. He pushed our "three-mile limit" of this world's shore line and opened up a way for us into the eternal dimensions of our existence. "He ascended into heaven." From the right hand of God, his clarion call to all who suffer and weep, to all who are lonely, afraid and defeated, is *Plus Ultra* — "There is more beyond." Until this *more* becomes a reality for us and to us and in us, we can never confess Christ as king.

The historic evidence of the Ascension is extremely limited in the New Testament; only the Book of Acts gives a detailed account. But what the Ascension of our Lord symbolizes and stands for, permeates to the heart of every word penned by the writers of the New Testament. These inspired men who wrote the Holy Scriptures were men enlightened and lifted up by the Risen and Ascended Lord. The perspective of the Ascension is the viewpoint from which they witnessed. They wrote *not* with fear-filled hearts and tear-filled eyes; they sang each word they wrote with hope and joy flooding every fiber of their beings. They had caught the vision of the ultimate victory of Christ, and they were messengers of a battle won and of a kingdom come. They saw beyond the man Jesus to the Messiah, beyond the stable to the sacred sanctuary, beyond the cross to the crown, beyond the tomb to the ultimate triumph.

Across the street from our seminary stands Ascension Lutheran Church. Above the altar is a stained glass window depicting the ascending Lord. The congregation decided to completely remodel the church sanctuary, but because of the sentimental attachment to the altar window, they decided to retain the ascension window in the new design.

When the remodeling was completed and the

congregation returned to the church sanctuary for worship, the little seven-year old son of the pastor leaned over to his mother and said, "A brand new church, but the same old Jesus."

This is the meaning of the Ascension for us: the same Jesus Christ ascended and thereby extended through all the changes of time and space.

When our Lord had completed his earthly ministry, he ascended to the Father, not to leave us, but in order that he might be constantly and unchangeably with us.

As our Ascended Lord occupies the chair of prophecy, we are assured by his ascension that false teachings will never ultimately mislead us. His word in Holy Scripture can never be permanently damaged by misunderstanding, for his Holy Spirit is constantly present to instruct and inspire his people to a continual reformation to preserve forever the faith of the gospel given to our fathers.

As our Lord occupies the chair of *priesthood*, no anxiety or doubt can overwhelm us, for we know that despite all adversaries, our Lord intercedes for us, pleading his sacrifice for our sins and imputing his innocence and righteousness to us. Because of Christ's Ascension, our "mourner's bench" becomes a "mercy seat" of every lasting joy.

As our Ascended Lord occupies the chair of *kingship*, we are assured that even when our society or the church is shattered by unrest, riot, or revolution, we can be comforted by the knowledge that Christ is ultimately in command. He is the King of Kings, and even the gates of hell shall not prevail against him.

Therefore, let us celebrate this Ascension Day with the words of Luther's hymn — "A Mighty Fortress Is Our God" — ringing in our ears. Let us sing out with gusto those stirring words, those prophetic words, those glory-filled words, "the right man on our side, the Man of God's own choosing."

Meanwhile we wait and work and witness and worship, knowing that one day every knee shall bow and every voice will proclaim him Lord, and we shall join the host of heaven and hail him, prophet, priest, and king!

The Wardrobe of God

SEVENTH SUNDAY OF EASTER
John 17:1-11

When you listened to the Gospel read this morning, you could hardly miss the fact that it was talking about glory.

It is not an easy passage of Scripture to understand at a first reading or hearing. It sounds deeply theological, and it is. The whole passage is deeply immersed in the theology of John who wrote it. This is compounded by the fact that John's use of the word "glory" does not compare with our common usage of the word. For example, let us examine some of the ways we employ the word "glory" in our ordinary speech.

First example:

I really resent him.
We do all the work;
he takes all the glory.

Here we are using the word "glory" as a status word of public praise. "Glory" is being well spoken of; it is an outstanding reputation. "Glory" is something we seek after, acquire, gain, either justly or unjustly.

Second example:

I am deeply moved
when I see "Old Glory"
pass in a parade.

Here we use the word "glory" to signify the honor and the respect we pay to the flag. It is not so much an opinion or status, as in the first example, but an emotion expressed for a symbol we hold in high regard.

Third example:

We went to the country club party last Saturday; it was a glorious affair.

Here the word "glory" is synonymous with splendid, magnificent, glamourous. It suggests something bright and dazzling.

Fourth example:

As a parent I really glory in my child's accomplishments.

This statement has a ring of personal pride in it, not for one's own self but for one close to you. It is an experience of admiration.

This brief survey suggests that we use the word "glory" in our everyday conversations to speak about something good, but not something associated or related to God.

When John uses the word "glory" in our lesson for this morning, he is not using it as we commonly use the word. He is using it exclusively as a characteristic of God, something that God, and God alone, possesses.

To understand what John means by the word "glory," it is necessary to go back into biblical history and see how the word developed. Alan Richardson, the New Testament scholar, gives us a hint of what to look for when he points out that the word "glory" in the Scriptures is born out of the experience of the *presence* of God on earth.

Running through both Old and New Testaments is a lively sense of the presence of God on earth dwelling among his people. This presence took a rich variety of forms — most of them anthropomorphic. For these primitive people could think only in terms of their own experiences. They believed that they were created in God's image and therefore God must look like them; but since he was holy, they were afraid to directly describe his looks in detail. Even Moses was permitted to see only the "back side" of God. Yet this did not detract in any way from their certainty that God was truly present in their lives.

Shrine

When God was present in a special way and communicated with his people, the place where he appeared became holy ground. In the story of Moses at the burning bush, God spoke, "Take off your sandals because you are standing on holy ground." (Exodus 3:5)

To remember these holy places, the people marked the spot by placing a stone or a pile of stones to form what today we would call an altar. When they desired to talk with God or offer sacrifices to him, they would return to this designated place. It became known as a shrine or a sanctuary.

Face

When worshipers went to these shrines, they said that they went to "see God's face." This did not mean they actually looked at God as one would look into a human face with nose and eyes and mouth; it was simply a way of indicating that God was making himself available in a very personal way. They could have an "audience" with God as people of their day would have come before their king. "The Face of God" became a common form of referring to God's presence; on the other hand, to say that God had turned his face away from them was a common form of expression to indicate that God had withdrawn his presence.

This form of God's presence as a "face" is reflected in the priestly benediction which is sometimes used to conclude a service of worship.

The Lord bless thee and keep thee.
The Lord make his face shine upon thee
and be gracious unto thee.
The Lord lift up his countenance upon thee
and give thee peace.

Ark

The Hebrews, however, were a mobile people — constantly on the move — so it was only natural that they would have a need for a portable shrine to represent God's presence among them. So the *ark* came into existence, which could be transported on their journeys. This ark served at least two functions. It was a receptacle in which the sacred stones containing the Ten Commandments could reside, and it also served as a *throne* for God himself. The ark was particularly convenient in times of war against their menacing neighbors. The ark enabled them to actually carry God with them into battle, thereby assuring them victory over their enemies.

The Temple

When the Hebrew people had secured the promised land and settled down to an established city and rural life, one of the first things they did was to build a temple to house the ark. This house of God with its ark became the national treasure embodying the history of Israel. It linked them with their sacred past and was a sign, not only of God's presence and his divine covenant with them as his chosen people, but also of the redemptive relationship which could not be broken between themselves and their God.

The Cloud

Strongly associated with the ark was another symbol of God's presence — a *cloud.* In their travels through the wilderness, the Israelites were guided by a pillar of smoke by day and of fire by night (Exodus 13:21). When they finally reached Canaan, God came down in the pillar of cloud and went inside the tent of the Tabernacle to talk with Moses.

The people recognized the cloud as the visible sign of God's presence (Exodus 33:7-11). The important thing is that the cloud thus came to be both a symbol of God's presence and a veil to hide his brilliance and power. All through their history, the Hebrews were concerned for the holiness and the transcendence of God, while at the same time rejoicing in his presence. They freely spoke of God's earthly presence but at the same time were constantly safeguarding his majesty and omnipotence — his holy-otherness.

Glory

Eventually all of these forms and images of God's earthly presence: the shrine, the face, the ark, the temple, the cloud, became focused in a single word — "glory."

The prophet Ezekiel was the first to use the term "glory" to express God's presence on earth. The actual word he used was *kabod,* which in Hebrew meant weight or substance. For example, a man of wealth wore distinctive clothing that reflected his wealth and power. Therefore, his outward appearance and bearing were his *kabod* — the outward sign of his power and prestige, and therefore demanded the respect and honor of all who saw him. Clothes did not make the man, as we frequently hear, as much as clothes reflected the man who "had it made." Hence weight, substance, wealth, power, dignity, nobility and honor were all suggested in the use of this single word *kabod — glory.*

Brightness

Ezekiel added the dimension of brightness to the word "glory" and spoke of God's presence as "a devouring fire on the top of a mountain." (Exodus 24:17)

When Moses descended from the Mount, his whole face shown with brightness because he had shared the brightness of God's glory.

This aspect of brightness related to God's glory is frequently used and in many cases takes on an eschatological aspect symbolizing life in the Kingdom of God both realized now and expected in the future. But the most dominant use of the word "glory" in the New Testament is in reference to Christ. The angels sang a song of glory at the birth of Christ, and it was echoed by the crowds at the Triumphal Entry into Jerusalem. The Fourth Evangelist especially stresses that the act of Christ's crucifixion was his hour of glory. Christ goes to the cross as a king to his crowning.

On earth the glory of God is revealed — made know in Jesus. When people looked at Jesus, they saw the glory — the presence of God. It is in the face of Christ that the light of the knowledge of the glory of God shines in our hearts with creative power (2 Corinthians 4:6). Christ made of Calvary a shrine for all times where heaven intersected the earth. Christ made of the cross an ark — a throne for God. His body became the new temple of God where all people might dwell together in peace.

In the entire New Testament, Christ is presented as the glory of God's presence made visible on earth to those whose eyes are open to see it; but perhaps it is in the Fourth Gospel that glory is most strongly stressed. John uses the Greek word *doxa,* which is translated as "glory," and there is little doubt that he used it with all the rich biblical background of the word in mind. For John, the word "glory" encompassed the shrine, the face, the ark, the cloud, the temple, the whole history of God's earthly presence with his people. All this comes to focus in the person of Jesus Christ. John forcefully proclaims in the very beginning of his Gospel: "We beheld his glory as of the only-begotten from the Father." (John 1:14)

In our Gospel lesson for this morning, John uses a form of the word glory six times in only ten verses. Christ glorifies the only true God on earth. The Father glorifies Christ. But perhaps — for us — the most significant statement of our whole Gospel lesson is the statement of Christ, *"I am glorified in them."*

Jesus is saying here that we — you and I — have been given the high privilege of glorifying God on earth. We have been chosen and called to the supreme status of being the means by which God's presence is made known today among all people. As Christ reflects the presence of God on earth, so we — in Christ — are to reflect and show forth the living presence of God on earth in our day.

In the sixth chapter of Judges, we have the story of an Old Testament hero named Gideon. The people of Israel were in one of their many periods of distress and disaster. They were being ruled over by the Midianites, and they felt that God had forsaken and deserted them.

In a dramatically-charged moment, an angel came to Gideon, greeting him with the words, "The Lord is with you, brave and mighty man."

Gideon said to him, "If I may ask you, sir, why has all this happened to us if the Lord is with us? What happened to all the wonderful things that our fathers told us the Lord used to do — how he brought them out of Egypt? The Lord has abandoned us and left us to the mercy of the Midianites."

Then the Lord ordered him, "Go with all your great strength and rescue Israel from the Midianites. I myself am sending you."

Gideon replied, "But, Lord, how can I rescue Israel? My clan is the weakest in the tribe of Manasseh, and I am the least important member of my family."

The Lord answered, "You can do it because I will help you." And the Lord did. With only one-hundred men, Gideon attacked and conquered the massive army of the Midianites, and the people of God were free.

A fascinating little detail of this story is found in verse 34 where the Scripture tells us that God took control of Gideon and gave him the power to fight and win his battle. In the American Standard version there is a marginal note at verse 34 which points out that what is literally being said here is, *God clothed himself with Gideon.* What a terrific image — God clothed himself with Gideon — and that is what our Lord meant in our text when he said, "I am glorified in them." God clothes himself with us. We are the clothing, the *wardrobe* God puts on to work his mighty works in our world in our day.

This is particularly striking as we remember that the origin of the word "glory" meant the garments worn by a rich and powerful man, and these garments reflect and show forth his wealth and power. Now Jesus is saying that we are God's glory; we are the clothes God puts on to show himself to the world. We are God's garments, God's clothes, God's wardrobe by which he shows his glory, himself, his presence to our world!

Every morning when we get up and put on our clothes to begin the day, we should remind ourselves that God wants us to be his *clothes, his wardrobe.* He wants our life to be his glory and show it forth. He wants our lives — what we say and do — to reflect his forgiveness, his generosity, his patience, his kindness, his care, his love for all people. What a challenge! What a calling!

There is a legend about a king of an early tribe that inhabited central Europe. He had twin sons and everyone wondered which boy would be chosen by the father to follow him as king.

When the boys reached maturity, the king called them to him. He held in his hand two royal rings — the sign and symbol of the king. He placed a ring on the finger of each of his sons, saying, "One of these is the genuine ring of the office of king and the other is a copy."

The sons looked at each other and then turned to their father, saying, "But if you die before telling the secret of which ring is genuine and which is the copy, how shall the people know who is to be their true and legal king?"

The old man reached out and held fast the hands of both his sons, and looking them straight in the eyes, he said, "The people will know who wears the genuine ring and therefore who is to be their king — by the way he lives."

We began the Easter Season with the account of the grave clothes our Lord left behind as he rose from the dead. Today we come to the end of the Easter Season with the message that Christ takes the *risen-clothes* of his glory and places them about our shoulders. As a patriarch of old placed the mantle of inheritance upon the shoulders of his chosen one, so Christ places the clothes of God's glory on us.

We wear the *wardrobe of God;* everyone who views our lives should be able to tell that among all people, we have been chosen to testify to the presence of God's love in our world.

Pray to God that he will be with us as he was with Gideon and will give us the power to wear the garments of new life, which our Lord has given us, to the constant glory of our God.